100 GREATEST COMIC BOOKS ™

By Jerry Weist

Historic Consultation and Introduction
By Jim Steranko

ACKNOWLEDGEMENTS

The depictions of the comic books identified in this book, including without limitation, copyrighted materials, characters, trademarks, service marks, trade names, and trade dress, are for the express purpose of identification and valuation. All copyrights, characters, trademarks, service marks, trade names, and trade dress are the property of their respective owners. All copyrights, characters, trademarks, service marks, trade names, and trade dress may not be copied or otherwise exploited without the permission of the owner(s) of such copyright, character, trademark, service mark, trade name, or trade dress. SPIDER-MAN, AMAZING FANTASY #15 TM & © 2004 Marvel Characters, Inc. Used with permission. Special thanks to Jim Steranko for the use of his text *The Ages of Comics* and *Ten Comics that Rocked the World*.

Art Direction: Matthew W. Jeffirs
Design: Robert A. Cashatt & Matthew W. Jeffirs
Editor: Teresa Lyle

Correspondence concerning this book's contents should be directed to the publisher:

3101 Clairmont Road

Suite C

Atlanta, Georgia 30329

www.whitmanpub.com

THE 100 GREATEST COMIC BOOKS

TABLE OF CONTENTS

I began reading comic books at my father's grocery store in Wichita, Kansas, when I took home copies of the early Pre-Hero Marvels. I also remember receiving a stack of about 60 late 1950s comics when I was very young and very sick. And I was one of the fortunate few (in the mid-west) who got to raid "Pop's" retail store basement in Concordia, Kansas, back when five cents would buy a comic dating to 1942, but you had to tolerate large brown paper tape attached to the spine! There are other pleasant memories of raiding Al's Old Book store, and the Pied Piper Bookstore in Wichita for back issues, and finding the occasional EC, Timely, or DC Golden Age book. And especially that rare day when Jack Whitesell took me into the back room of his bookstore and said, "Young man you have all summer to pay for these, and it's six for a quarter." What was there? Seven boxes of every single DC and Marvel Silver Age comic in essentially Very Fine Plus to Near Mint. Included in this horde were all the Marvel Pre-Hero Fantasy and DC Science Fiction Fantasy titles from about 1958 with a few early issues of SHOWCASE missing, including, sadly, the No. 4, and FANTASTIC FOUR No. 1, to the end of 1963. I was thirteen years old, and my comic collecting days were about to begin. If I had told my parents that one day a comic book would sell for over $100,000 or that perfect file copies of ECs from the 1950s (just over ten years old then!) would sell for thousands of dollars each, well, it would have been more far fetched than if I had told them that "men will someday land on the moon!"

It's been nearly forty years since that time; I've grown up, and the comics industry and comic collecting have grown up too. What was once an insider's hobby is now a multi-million dollar a year business, with people collecting everything from early Yellow Kid premiums, to near mint condition comic books, to original comic book art, to the hundreds of books published about comic history itself! When I was asked to author this book, my first question was "why hasn't this book been done before?"

Part of the reason may be that so many specific histories on the comics have surfaced during the past twenty years that authors tended to overlook the larger picture. And part of the reason may be simply that no one wanted to take on the arduous task. But having authored two comic art price guides, I figured I had already experienced first hand the questions that would await me! I await these inevitable words: "How could you leave that book out?"

I'm in debt to Jim Steranko and Bruce Hamilton who took special consideration and time in the early stages of this book to advise me on my listing of criteria, and how to organize and execute the voting ballots. Jim also wrote the wonderful introduction to this book, "The Ten Comics That Rocked America." Steranko's special "The Ages of Comics" (which should give us comic veterans all pause, and food for thought) is also published here for the first time. Jim has been an inspiration to work with; he contributed input to my own writing and kept me from going off track on several occasions. Bruce Hamilton also sent me historical perspectives (he wrote the bio on MICKEY MOUSE MAGAZINE), as did John Snyder of Diamond Galleries. My primary editor, Christopher Boyko, is responsible for cleaning up my writing, correcting any historical mistakes I made, and drawing attention to important perspectives for certain comics. Chris also wrote the script for eight books, including THE WATCHMEN and FANTASTIC FOUR No. 48. Roger Hill wrote the original description for MOTION PICTURE FUNNIES No. 1 that appeared in the 1993 Sotheby's Comic Art Catalogue that is adapted here. Jim Steranko wrote the HOT ROD COMICS nn entry, and I had input from Tony Davis for ALL-NEGRO COMICS No. 1.

I'm also very much indebted to each and every single voter. This is a small list, but the names that are there represent a major portion of the history of comics fandom, and I'm proud to say that this list is a very balanced group of professionals, fans, and comic book dealers. They each offered me specific information, encouragement, and took the time to seriously consider their choices.

If you've never before collected or read comic books, congratulations for having the curiosity and interest to purchase this volume. But words of warning: comics are habit forming! What begins with a simple desire to read and learn soon turns into a passion to own and discover! Take it from one who knows, and doesn't regret a moment, year, decade, or lifetime of comic book reading and collecting.

Jerry Weist

When I was growing up, there were only a few things that kids could claim exclusively as their own: rock and roll, pegged pants, shoes called fruit boots, *American Bandstand*, souped-up cars, zip guns, and comic books.

It wasn't much, but that was all we had–and those with the presence of mind to hang onto their comics very possibly took an early retirement in Palm Springs. Ironic that the cheapest , most disposable entertainment format outstripped everything else to become a high-priced annuity in the collectible market.

Before my folks threw out my comics, I used them for a secondary purpose: they were the art school I could never afford to attend. I studied comics, educated myself regarding draftsmanship, perspective, and rendering. Then, I learned composition and design from old magazines, and storytelling from the movies. I was a culture junkie who absorbed his craft the hard way. In retrospect, the process may have been the most gratifying in my childhood.

Comics left an indelible stamp on my creative persona and, because you're reading this book, they probably had a similar effect on you, too. Good or bad, comics were a significant part of our collective cultural experience and this book celebrates that quality in a very specific manner: by articulating key moments in the history of the four-color chronology. Whether you were there when they originally materialized on newsstands or are experiencing them for the first time, you'll find that the 100 examples showcased here perfectly capture the essence of the form.

Just for the record, I'd like to define that form because there seems to be some misunderstanding about its fundamental qualities. I am aware there are currently a myriad of variations available, but I'm referring specifically to the traditional comic book, which is:

- a full-color booklet approximately 7 x 10" in size

- containing passages of related line-art panels positioned sequentially

- and expressing dialogue and thoughts in balloons

Anything else is a *mutation*. If the color element is removed, the item becomes a B&W comic book. Change the size to 5 x 7, and it becomes a digest comic book. Substitute the line-art panels with photographs and you have a *fumetti* comic book. Increase the number of pages and it becomes a fat comic book. Eliminate the balloons and it becomes an oddball item with no clear definition, beyond what might be loosely termed an illustrated book. Dramatic content or subject matter is not a consideration; neither is price, the publisher's imprint, the quality of the stock, the manner of binding, nor the treatment of the line-art style.

Considering the simplicity of the form, it's surprising that comics required decades to develop into a package with the above-named elements. But, as historians note, combinations of text and images have been printed since the invention of the press, and even produced before that in handcrafted editions. That ontogeny has been well-documented and some of the major entries will be found in this book. While the experts wrangle over the details, let's focus momentarily on an area rarely covered in overviews of comic book history, a direction that sparked the title of this essay: comics that were so influential that they changed the nature of the form.

The concept occurred to me about a decade ago and triggered a search into the labyrinth of the four-color dreamscape. It was easy to spot the obvious contenders NEW FUN 1, ACTION 1, MAD 1 and a handful of others—but for every one that was easily spotted, there was another, virtually hidden in the Niagara of newsprint pages published in the past seventy years. Influential is the key word and, as any student of the comic book will verify, few, if any, have actually had an authentic impact on the field.

Certainly CAPTAIN AMERICA 1 would be on everyone's list of their 100 greatest comics (especially if they actually read it as a WW2 youth) because the character struck a resonant chord, in addition to spawning a battalion of patriotic wannabees. But the book is on my TCTRTW list for a completely different reason: essentially that Jack Kirby showed the world—and expressly the brotherhood of comic book artists—how explosive and epigrammatic a superhero could, and should, be.

If you don't believe it, compare his early Captain America (issues 1-10) to early Superman; the difference is that between a Jane Fonda aerobics workout and an Ali-Fraser championship fight. The Man of Steel posed passively as a salvo of .50 caliber bullets bounced off his chest. Conversely, when Cap burst into action, muscles that never appeared on any anatomy chart suddenly distended, elongated, and jackhammered with so much superhuman power that readers could feel the aftershock.

Sure, Kirby had previously drawn Blue Bolt, Red Raven, Mercury, and a handful of other heroes, but none with the atomic-powered conviction with which he envisioned comics' quintessential Sentinel of Liberty. For sheer dynamism, no character could compete with Captain America–but they tried! Kirby set a terrifying creative pace that few artists could equal and that none has ever beaten, even a half century later. Kirby was comics' first shockwave penciller. He ignited a generation of imitators with the first issue of a seminal character with whom he would be identified forever.

It's interesting that the three *most* influential artists on the comics field were not in the business at all, but allied in a neighboring forum: the newspaper comic strip. Perhaps 90% or more of all comics illustrators, until about 1970, spun off in some configuration of Milton Caniff (Terry and the Pirates), Hal Foster (Prince Valiant) and Alex Raymond (Flash Gordon). Even Kirby.

Comics' Golden Age rippled with stylists—Lou Fine, Mort Meskin, Joe Kubert, Mac Raboy, C.C. Beck, Jack Cole, Bill Everett, Bob Powell, H.G. Peter, Alex Schomberg, and others—but, besides Kirby, none had a profound influence among their peers until Reed Crandall emerged as the finest draftsman in comics, a position he maintained until a decade or so before his death in 1982.

While Kirby derived his raw power from a formula that mixed equal parts cartoon with realism, Crandall was a consummate realist. His early period (1941-43), however (visualizing Uncle Sam, The Ray, Firebrand, and even Blackhawk), was typified by a lighter, broader approach. The turnaround, surprisingly, did not materialize at Quality Comics, but at Fiction House with a 12-page Kaanga story in JUNGLE 42 (6/43).

Though forgotten by today's collectors, the standout story coalesced Crandall's figure work with an idiosyncratic action style, an illustrator's penchant for panel composition, and an impeccably-mature inking approach (it was so good that Eisner is still using it). The result was a breathtaking *tour de force* that stunned artists, inkers, and editors, and set a new standard for the form.

Essentially, Crandall's example confirmed that first-rate art was possible even with the most clichéd material. Pencillers bought two copies: one to read and another to cut up and add to their swipe files–even veteran Wally Wood returned to the Kaanga morgue numerous times, including for his '60s mosquito-opera Animan. Crandall's heroic anatomy, from Blackhawk to Captain Triumph and beyond, informed the work of others for decades that followed.

Wood, of course, admitted to many influences, but if any comics artist was born with an idiosyncratic creative vision, he would be the one. A child prodigy with pencil and paper, he produced a myriad of unusually-expressive, hand-made comics throughout his school years and, after a WW2 tour in the Merchant Marine and another in the Paratroopers, found his vocation in the field he loved most: comics. Primarily self-taught, he worked briefly for several publishers, then joined the EC staff in Spring 1950. His earliest efforts reflected a cartoony approach he had learned copying Disney material and newspaper adventure strips, but, within a single year, he not only found a personal artistic direction, but also transformed his diverse bag of tricks into a powerfully cohesive style the elevated him to the number one spot in the EC bullpen, a group of young Turks bristling with talent.

With each successive story, Wood hit a new plateau, finally finding an astounding groove with "Gray Cloud of Death" in WEIRD SCIENCE 9 (9/51). His spaceship interiors (a combination of B-29 and submarine housings), costumes (part *Buck Rogers*, part *Destination Moon*), aliens (inspired by medical diagrams of inner–body parts), rockets (Willy Ley and the pulp artists), and galactic voids (Chesley Bonstell) merged with rich blacks (Caniff) lush females (Raymond), and dramatic, double-lit figures (Foster) to push comic art into a new universe–one laminated with layers of audience-pleasing Zip-a-Tone.

Wood took readers where no man had gone before. He made science fiction exotic (especially in his quintessential statement "My World") with a wild combination of techno-ordnance and barbaric bric-a-brac, all rendered with a genuinely magical line that could change any penciller's work into a Wood masterpiece. And he excelled in every genre, from humor to horror. The impact of his SF work resonated powerfully in the comics world and through those who made their living in it; no one has yet to do it better.

Influence on one's contemporaries is one thing; influencing an entire genre is another. Alex Toth has done both. A natural draftsman with a phenomenal penchant for narrative orchestration, he was an accomplished pro while still in his teens, brandishing a style that nodded to comic strip aces Milt Caniff, Noel Sickles, Roy Crane, and magazine illustrator Robert Fawcett, among others. Toth's artistic vision, however, mitigated his inspiration foundations and–like an actor who learns his lines, then forgets them—he delivered decades of virtuoso work as original as it was exciting.

Beginning at DC in mid-1947, Toth put his own brand on a series of characters, including Green Lantern, Sierra Smith, and particularly notable run of Johnny Thunder in ALL-AMERICAN WESTERN, in addition to a handful of romance and SF tales. While he brought sophisticated illustrative approaches to them all, it was his contemporary material—such as the BIG TOWN covers and DANGER TRAIL yarns—that had a galvanizing effect on the DC art staff. Together with Dan Barry, who worked on THE ADVENTURES OF ALAN LADD and GANG BUSTERS and embraced a similar artistic philosophy, Toth was responsible for what could be termed the '50s DC house style, one that prevailed for decades afterward.

He had a similar influence at Standard during the same era and it was during this period that he also defined a genre (a slightly less judicious viewpoint might state he *created* the genre). Toth's predilection for aviation material is obvious from today's perspective (BRAVO FOR ADVENTURE) and was one of his major projects in the past few decades). But in 1950, there was only the Caniff-Sickles connection to inform us—until his work in FRONTLINE COMBAT. Toth drew only two tales for the magazine–*Thunder Jet* (issue 8) and F-86 *Sabre Jet* (issue 12)–yet with those stories, he transcended every aeronautic mission flown in comics to that point.

In the first (obviously laid out by editor Harvey Kurtzman), the aircraft itself became the story's protagonist, while Toth's clean, ingenuous treatment was almost shocking in a book that exploited extensive detail. (It was followed by Wood's "Caesar," with its armies of thousands, all back-lit and Zip-a-Toned). The second tale took a similar direction, but with considerably less Kurtzman input. Toth's use of negative space was exhilarating. White clouds drifted in yellow skies *without* holding lines. The few faces actually seen were enclosed in oxygen masks and helmets. Both efforts were confirmed kills! Toth had found a different way to articulate air-war action and was frequently imitated afterward in aviation titles, yet his status as comics' Ace of Aces was never topped. Toth raised the creative bar of the four-color format as high as anyone in its 70-year history.

A much different approach to comic narrative can be attributed to Charles Biro, a triple-threat heavyweight who often wrote, drew, and edited his comics' efforts. Beginning a career in 1936 at the Harry "A" Chesler shop, he initially focused on cartoon strips featuring elflike characters rendered with an unusually delicate line (interesting because Biro was a tall, massive individual). As the decade ended, he migrated to MLJ, where he wrangled a group of titles predicated on high adventure and superheroes. Less than two years later, he moved to Lev Gleason Publications and shaped a series of books with less editorial restrictions and more than a touch of sensationalism.

Biro was a creative dynamo that immediately launched DAREDEVIL and BOY COMICS, both of which still qualify as offbeat offerings. He also initiated CRIME DOES NOT PAY 22 (6/42), generally targeted as the first major crime book, an honor celebrated in the *100 Greatest* listing but mentioned here because of the radical literary and artistic direction that Biro invested in it. The book's specific "true crime" approach immediately isolated it from a few earlier contenders, such as GANG BUSTERS, because its stories were usually told from the criminals' viewpoint. The formula was repeated with CRIME AND PUNISHMENT 1 (4/48).

Under Biro's supervision, tales were stripped of melodramatic heroism, which was replaced with realistic, street-tough dialogue and gritty art. Handsome G-men and muscular dicks were supplanted by greasy hoods and pock-marked killers. The best narratives eschewed the devices of virtuoso storytelling and instead went for a documentary approach that was well stated by vets George Tuska and Fred Guardineer: eye-level medium shots, few angles, minimal movement, no dramatic lighting, and bleak backgrounds. The pedestrian, anti-art treatment contrasted brutally with the violent subject matter in the stories. Balloons and captions were frequently so dense they obscured half or more of every panel. If there was a word to describe the direction, it would lie somewhere between nasty, perverse, and just plain ugly—but it worked!

That approach was always captured by the cover art, a conceit mandated by Biro's ego. He alone dominated the covers of Gleason's two crime titles. His realistic style was reminiscent of that of fine artist George Grosz, replete with moles, bad teeth, and other imperfections. Biro spurned idealism on covers and his often awkward figures—bloodied, beaten, and brutalized—looked more like *Daily News* crime scene photos than comic book illustrations. And should anyone miss the point of who was in charge, he inevitably signed every cover with a Number 5 sable brush in letters so large they often matched some words in the magazine's title. Charles Biro was the first personality to emerge from the comics arena.

While it may be redundant to list Kirby twice on the TCTRTW roster, it's entirely appropriate because he was responsible for two distinct trends in two distinct eras. Exactly twenty years after the birth of Captain America he visualized FANTASTIC FOUR 1 (11/61) and jumpstarted a new look that would typify comics for decades to come. Remarkably, it was not only how he drew, but *what he drew!* Although the elements in FF were present in his earlier work, Kirby transformed them into a leitmotif that gave the book its idiosyncratic personality. Rather than using mechanical props and high-tech backgrounds as decorative subtexts in his stories, Kirby elevated them to primary status, often as important and inimitable as the characters themselves. Readers referred to the hardware as "Kirby machinery" and no one in comics ever did it better.

It took Kirby about a dozen issues to *find* the superheroic team artistically and intellectually, and maybe another half year to engulf them in the technoscapes that became *de rigueur* for the series. Afterward, vistas of fantastic mechanica abounded; wall-sized electronic consoles, galactic animatrons, futuristic weaponry, robotic warrior-gods, and psychotronic gimmicks became an integral part of the series matrix, a hotwired amalgam that supercharged readers as well as other Marvel bullpenners and competitive wannabees.

In addition, Kirby perfected an architectonic vision that allowed him to create unbelievable urban landscapes with relative ease, using a Lego-like approach similar to his biomechanical formula. Nicknamed "The King," he ignited comics techno-wars and short-circuited the status quo to become the most imitated artist in the last half of the 20th Century–and possibly ever.

A competitive runner up behind Kirby, Neal Adams picked up the overflow as the second most imitated artist of the era. His primary strength was his superb draftsmanship, an uncanny ability to draw the human figure in any imaginable position and often fearlessly foreshortened (an aspect that often separates the men from the boys in Comicbookland). Adams also excelled in emotional expressions like few others in the panel business and his characters inevitably exuded dramatic heat. Taking the point one step further, he specialized in angst, and somewhere in all his narratives, Adams' heroes would burst into a paroxysm of raw angst, savage angst, venomous angst, bloodthirsty angst, or a number of other angsts that defy description. Readers loved it!

Adams' style was heavily influenced by Lou Fine, John Prentice, and Stan Drake (on whose respective newspaper strips *Peter Scratch*, *Rib Kirby*, and *Juliet Jones*, he worked. His pen and brush line was the most volatile and ecstatic in the field: organic, rich, and so energetic it pulled readers into stories with breathtaking persuasion. Although he charted the *Ben Casey* comic strip for two years and made numerous forays into comics, it was not until he answered the necrophillic call of Deadman in STRANGE ADVENTURES 206 (11/67) that fans and fellow artists felt his impact.

Adams followed with a series of bull's-eyes on Green Arrow, Green Lantern, X-Men, Batman, and other heroes, each of which inspired a new league of lookalikes. When self-publishing became an option, he formed Continuity Comics and released a volley of titles, all predicated on his panache and popularity. Adams and his clones, now several generations removed, continue making their presence felt in the field.

As comics bounced from decade to decade, two aspects of the form, once as inseparable as conjoined twins, began to diverge. Until the 1960s, art and storytelling were the heart and soul of comics, but when fanboys (readers turned pros) infiltrated the business, art became predominant, while storytelling was relegated to a subordinate position. The adolescent focus on lines on paper threw the spotlight on numerous stylists, in addition to a few first-rank illustrators. John Buscema was one of the latter.

When Crandall exited the field as its premiere anatomist, Buscema inherited the top spot. Ironically, his career, which began in the 1940s, languished during the next two decades, while he produced a mountain of undistinguished work, mostly crime, romance, and Westerns. Although he eventually became a skilled illustrator, his lack of interest in narrative technique resulted in the mundane quality of his panel-to-panel orchestration. It wasn't until Stan Lee gave him a stack of Kirby comics and explained the facts of life that Buscema added vitality and continuity to his approach. Studying Kirby's exaggerated action and narrative devices, Buscema turned his style around almost overnight. The effect was immediately apparent in his four-issue run beginning with AVENGERS 41 (6/67).

He had turned over a new leaf and everyone knew it, though they may not have comprehended the reason why. Brandishing his Kirbyized style like a battle-ax, Buscema cut a prodigious path through the Marvel universe, proving that it was possible to match quantity with quality. He revived SUB-MARINER (5/68) from the depths of comic oblivion, polished SILVER SURFER (8/68) to masterpiece sheen in seventeen spectacular issues, and thrust CONAN (4/73) to a pinnacle of popularity undreamed of by Barry Smith. Buscema reigned as comics' quintessential draftsman until his death in 2002.

The current emphasis on artists is so obsessive that other talents are often overlooked, even when they establish new precedents in the form. Scott Williams is one of those talents. Often eclipsed by the superstars with whom he collaborated, his contribution has nonetheless reached an unparalleled zenith in the art of comics inking. As a capable penciller with less assignment than he required, Williams opted to ink the work of others and began refining the process using stringent intellectual control and machinelike discipline over an impeccable line. The result was a pioneering effort that perfected a series of new devices to delineate shapes and textures on the comics page, a feat no American inker had accomplished in three-quarters of a century.

In less than a decade, Williams was at the top of his form, using split feathering, open triangles, graduated strokes defining light-to-dark strata, and other over-rendering tricks with a sterile, unemotional line that set a demanding precedent for a regiment of rise-and-thrall runners-up. The big score eluded him, however, until a series of elements aligned in X-MEN 268 (10/90). Writer Chris Claremont had rallied the title's audience for a long run of solid scripts and, in this issue, structured a Captain America/Black Widow/Wolverine team-up that became the retail hot-ticket of the month. Although they had witnessed Williams' ascent as a major inker for years, readers finally became aware of his artistic integrity by sheer exposure to the key X-Men issue. He has since become the highest-paid inker in comics, with no plan to relinquish the position anytime soon.

Since the dawn of comics almost a century ago, no foreign stimulus has ever influenced the American product—until recently. Unlike many overseas countries which import comics, the United States (except for reprints in HEAVY METAL and a few other magazines) is essentially a self-sustaining operation. In fact, for years, European comics were a turn-off to Yankee readers. Nevertheless, manga (Japanese comics) has become commonplace in bookstores and on newsstand nationwide.

The reason for its acceptance harkens back to the 1960's TV cartoonmania and series such as KIMBA THE WHITE LION, SPEED RACER, and ASTRO BOY. After decades of cathode indoctrination (which includes millions of speed lines and easily as many tonsils), several generations of American audiences were slowly acclimated to Japanese animation style and content. But the comics audience held out until the English-language publication of AKIRA (9/88). Epic Comics 38-issue series, about violent biker gangs in a post-apocalyptic Japan encountering a mysterious psychic force, was hard-edged science fantasy, galaxies apart from the cute, Saturday-morning animation on which audiences had grown up.

Bombarded by manga on newsstands and anime on film and TV, American artists began to adapt and assimilate the identifying elements–large eyes, small noses and mouths, speed lines, thin teen characters, biorobotic armor, schoolgirl babes with big guns and bigger breasts–into their own work. Others have borrowed themes–tapping sources from *Seven Samurai* to LONE WOLF AND CUB—and shoehorned them into overground assignments. Even Japanese plastic model and movie production art magazines, such as *New Type* and *Hobby Japan* have had a significant impact on comics' creators. Taking a step back, it seems apparent that anime has had a much greater influence on the field than the Japanese comics themselves, confirming that the form continues to be more of a cultural barometer than its detractors realize.

These are ten comics that rocked the world, And one final clarification about my title: I meant the comic world, of course. Bet you knew it all along.

JIM STERANKO

Clocking from the earliest qualifying periodical features and strips, comics are a century old and, like jazz, still one of the few authentic American art forms. The exhilarating amalgam of words and images structured in a narrative format pioneered by the Yellow Kid, Little Nemo, and other characters, generated a tidal wave of cartoonmania that engulfed the world's imagination, tickled its funnybone, and ultimately synthesized a medium for expanded expression.

Although an industry emerged from the concept, its leaders have failed to adequately guide-line the form's evolution, particularly in its native environment. Considering the omission, it does not seem inappropriate, at this point, to define a functional chronology and terminology for the significant movements in comics history.

THE ELEMENTAL AGE: 1400-1897

The modern comic book evolved from a myriad of sources, dating back to the handcrafted woodcut that figured in the invention of the printing press. After movable type (circa 1450) was developed, allowing a greater quality and quantity of book production, the use of illustrations became more commonplace, including cartoons and caricatures. European periodicals regularly featured single-panel drawings, but it was not until the 1800s that they exploited word balloons and were commonly placed in narrative sequences. In 1842, THE ADVENTURES OF OBADIAH OLDBUCK appeared in a 40-page B&W magazine (saddle-stitched like modern comics) featuring 195 panels (but without balloons and color). A host of American humor magazines, such as *Puck* (1877), *Judge* (1881), and *Life* (1883), developed configurations of the standard comic book elements during this period—but, like the Euro originals, they were all for adults.

THE FORMATIVE AGE: 1897-1933

Begins with the YELLOW KID IN MCFADDEN'S FLATS (1897), a 5 $^1/_2$ x 7 $^1/_2$" 196-page book with a color cover and B&W interiors, essentially focusing on a single character and reprinting Sunday newspaper pages from the *New York World*. In the following three decades, Buster Brown, the Katzenjammer Kids, Foxy Grandpa, Happy Hooligan, and others follow suit with a multitude of formats, from tabloid to hardbound. The comics foundation is established, but the structural supports are still outstanding.

THE REPRINT AGE: 1933-1938

Begins with FUNNIES ON PARADE (1933), a 32-page, full-color giveaway that circulated a million copies and, along with the 64-page FAMOUS FUNNIES: A CARNIVAL OF COMICS (1934) that retailed for a dime, is responsible for establishing a newsstand market for comic-strip reprints. A host of imitations follow, some with original material (because it was cheaper than paying newspaper-strip syndicate rates), yet none that has significant impact on readers. But the size, style, and substance are aligned and awaiting a new direction—which isn't long in coming.

THE GOLDEN AGE: 1938-1947

Begins with ACTION 1 (6/38) and ignites the first superhero explosion indigenous to comics. The appearance and subsequent success of Superman points the way for a multitude of cloaked and cowled mimics, variant titles, and new publishing companies exploiting the trend. Often using WW2 as a rallying point, the movement is dominated by a legion of colorful and often bizarre heroes of every persuasion— with some press runs in the millions. The standard comic book format is clearly established (in this period, a dime buys 64 pages of comics) and popularized to the point of being a household item. For the first time in publishing history, kids not only have their own magazines in their own newsstand racks, but also they have them in a unique format, as functional as it is affordable.

THE SYNTHETIC AGE: 1947-1956

Begins with YOUNG ROMANCE (9/47) and a flood of love, science fiction, horror, crime, and Western titles—plus a new kind of humor comic. After a decade of phenomenal sales and substantial profits, all but the most popular characters fade away as the formula fantasies of the '40s are eclipsed by the reality-steeped '50s. The comics are growing up. When the superhero franchise collapses, they are forced to diversify and find raw material in hot rods, military combat, monsters, pirates, animals, private eyes, swashbucklers, and the supernatural, in addition to TV-related content. The new direction is fascinating, but too frail to support its own weight. Page counts are cut in half, from 64 to 32, but the price remains the same. In 1954, fallout from Senate hearings investigating the link between juvenile delinquency and comics—and the resulting Comics Code Authority—reduces the number of titles from about 650 to *less than half* and counting. Comics are caught in a publishing depression and need a creative transfusion to survive.

THE REVIVAL AGE: 1956-1961

Begins with SHOWCASE 4 (10/56) and recasts established superheroes for a new audience. Only a small group of publishers survive the crisis as sales plummet, creating a lethal struggle to find another direction. An updated Flash is the first to be reincarnated and is followed by other DC tryout retreads—Green Lantern, Hawkman, and the Atom—plus a revived Justice Society aka Justice League. Readers are receptive, but when other outfits try to compete with spies, sci-fi guys, and strong men, the results are unsuccessful. Instead, staffs are downsized. More titles are dropped. The body count escalates on Comics Row.

THE MARVEL AGE: 1961-1977

Begins with FANTASTIC FOUR 1 (11/61) and infuses contemporary characterization with techno-plots. Attempting to forge a rival version of the Justice League, Stan Lee and Jack Kirby create the FF and discover a prototype formula of part superpower, part philosophy, and part psychosis, a four-color equation of Shakespearean dimensions that is subsequently applied to the Hulk, Spider-Man, Thor, Ant-Man, Iron Man, the Avengers, X-Men, and a legion of others, who magnetically attract a hipper, older audience to the comics universe. Have no fear, the heroes have returned!

THE INDEPENDENT AGE: 1977-1985

Begins with CEREBUS 1 (1977) and embraces alternative publishing, distribution, and the comic-shop phenomenon. After the first comic convention in NYC in 1965, collectors-turned-dealers are responsible for the growth of specialty shops nationwide during the following decades. Until this point, national magazine distributors had a headlock on comics' circulation, but a direct-to-retail outlet system is created, allowing small, maverick independents to enter the field and compete with mainstream product. Eventually, the shops became the primary outlets for all comics publishers. Come back again real soon, y'hear—comics will be in next Wednesday!

THE DIGITAL AGE: 1985-PRESENT

Begins with SHATTER 1 (6/85) and employs computer-generated art, digitally-rendered color, and electronic production techniques. For the previous half century, comic books were colored using a functional, but extremely limited (in terms of tonal graduations and rendering effects) method involving overlays and multiple exposures during the platemaking stage of reproduction. Sophisticated computer programs revolutionize the procedure and allow creators not only to contribute to, but control the coloring process, in addition to manipulating scanned art, adding textures, lettering, and applying imaginative special effects to the work. Hello, Photoshop!

What lies beyond the horizon for comics? My guess is a variety of electronic formats. Thirty years ago, I was asked what I saw in comics' future and responded with a vision about a fan visiting his neighborhood entertainment emporium and buying something as small as an aspirin from a display card on the front counter. Outside, he reaches into his back pocket and unrolls a flexible monitor screen, just like it was an old magazine. The kid punches the pill into a tiny slot and the screen lights up, music begins to play, and characters come to life with startling reality. Welcome to THE ELECTRONIC AGE OF COMICS!

WHAT IS THE GREATEST AMERICAN COMIC BOOK?

One of the first questions new collectors ask is: "What is the greatest American comic book?"

The answer to this question is universally acknowledged to be ACTION COMICS No. 1. The character of Superman (first introduced in ACTION COMICS No. 1), created by Jerry Siegel and Joe Shuster, jumpstarted the comic book industry from an experimental stage to the mass market phenomena that it is today. This single comic book has stood the test of time throughout the comic's short history and is ranked as the single most important comic book.

WHAT MAKES A COMIC BOOK GREAT?

Greatness is subjective. However, the criteria for inclusion in *The 100 Greatest Comic Books* are listed below.

HISTORICAL IMPACT

How did a comic book change the industry; or how did it change the course of history in comics? First appearances should not take precedent over historical impact. An example of this would be CAPTAIN AMERICA No. 1 vs. PEP COMICS No. 1 (with the first patriotic hero). The Simon and Kirby superhero Captain America captured the imagination of the public and became the real "trend setter," where PEP COMICS No. 1 with The Shield, after many years simply holds the title of first patriotic hero comic book. The Yellow Kid, on the other hand, was the first American comic character, and he changed history as well.

QUALITY -The title of this book says greatest and this implies editorial and artistic and creative "greatness."

Again, it is not necessarily "the first of its kind," where Gold Key's THE MAN FROM U.N.C.L.E. No. 1 might come before Marvel's NICK FURY AGENT OF S.H.I.E.L.D. No.1; it is Steranko's artwork and concept that have had the lasting effect on comics. Quality extends itself to artistic greatness, editorial excellence, and the level of creativity found in new writers.

INTRODUCTION OF NEW CONCEPTS -What caused lasting change in the comic book industry with the introduction of new concepts? ACTION COMICS No. 1 brought about the change from newspaper reprint comics to the introduction of superheroes, and ignited the Golden Age of comics. MAD No. 1 revolutionized the comic industry, and ZAP COMICS No. 1 turned it over again a decade and a half later. Later on, new writers such as Neil Gaiman and Alan Moore brought into the industry the first great graphic novel concepts.

RARITY -It is important to acknowledge rarity, as well as value in collecting. Many times the most important comic books are also the most expensive. However, the criteria for including comics in this book are based on cultural concerns; this book is not a price guide count down for the 100 most expensive comic books.

Rarity and value are considerations given to the total picture of a comic's impact on the field.

CRITERIA

POPULARITY -Great comic books are bought and saved and read by a wide audience of people. Many of the greatest comic books included in this volume have also been on record as the largest selling, such as WALT DISNEY'S COMICS & STORIES, CAPTAIN MARVEL ADVENTURES, SUPERMAN, and THE X-MEN. Popularity can also be a trap, and the voters for this volume usually stuck with the first three listed criteria, over the last two, in making their final decisions.

CHOOSING AMERICA'S 100 GREATEST COMIC BOOKS

Making the choice for the 100 greatest comic books was a difficult process. The problem was resolved by the author making an initial listing that included his choice for the 135 greatest comic books. The voters were then asked to eliminate 35, and they were given the space to include fifteen comics of their own choosing. They could either eliminate the unwanted 35 down to 100, or eliminate up to 50 titles, and write in their choices for the fifteen additions.

Foreign comics were not included. Many of the early Victorian age square bound and hardcover comic books were also not included. Very recent comics with no evidence of their historical impact on the comics industry were also not included. The primary field of consideration was the 64-page, full-color comic book for a dime.

The remarkable fact is that the majority of voters eliminated most of the very same books off the original listing of 135! And these same voters were also responsible for correcting the author's omissions, with such outstanding examples as FANTASTIC FOUR No. 48, and THE SPIRIT WEEKLY COMIC BOOK. In the end, a kind of comic logic took over, and the final 100 stand listed.

HOW DID THE AUTHOR CHOOSE THE RANKING OF COMIC BOOKS?

Here, of course, the answer is that where sane men feared (at risk of loss of life) to tread, the author was a sucker for the bait! It is apparent to anyone reading this book with just the fundamentals of comics history that many important comics were not included. It is also apparent that you may choose to draw cards for each included comic, throw them up into the air, have them land in a pile, and come up with a ranking that you could then defend.

The consensus of the voters held very well for the top 25 titles, but then it broke down into a game of favorites, or the juxtaposition of differing values. Having to rank the comic book titles for the format of this book (with the more important being given more space) forced the author to make a choice to rank all 100. So remember that after about No. 25 it's a historical open book to how you rank the importance of each comic book.

THE RESULTS -The results then are a combination of the above process. As acknowledged in the author's introduction, Bruce Hamilton and Jim Steranko had important conceptual introductory ideas for the author's consideration. The voters themselves, however, gave this book its greatest value; their combined knowledge, experience, and love of the comics' medium have throughout the years caused comics not to be forgotten.

VOTER ACKNOWLEDGMENTS

**LISTING OF VOTERS FOR THE *100 GREATEST COMIC BOOKS*
PROFESSIONAL COMICS WRITERS, ARTISTS, COLLECTORS AND DEALERS**

The comics market is made up and defined by a number of different groups of individuals. Each group is important to the continuing development of the comic book industry. Comics' fandom began in the late 1950s, became focused enough to have conventions by the mid-1960s, and gained force throughout the 1970s and 1980s. Without fandom, the thousands of fanzines and professional historical books written about the history of comics would have never been produced. The professional writers and artists within the industry were 80% originally from fandom, and now continue as pros to develop the medium. Comic book dealers play an important role as well, and their excavations of America's past continue to this day to enrich the known holdings of old and rare comic books. The voting done for this book therefore was done by a combination of these groups, and their results give a more balanced look at the rich culture inherent within the comics themselves.

VOTING LIST

Last	First	Last	First
Alexander,	David	Kochman,	Charles
Bails,	Jerry G.	Levitz,	Paul
Benson,	John	Mannerino,	Joe
Berk,	Jon	Margolin,	Howard
Borock,	Steve	Matetsky,	Harry
Boyko,	Christopher	Naiman,	Michael
Crain,	Glynn	Nolan,	Michelle
Davis,	Tony	Overstreet,	Bob
Edwards,	Bruce	Payette,	James
Ellison,	Harlan	Petty,	John E.
Evanier,	Mark	Plant,	Bud
Feldstein,	Albert	Rogovin,	Robert
Flynn,	Peter	Shelly,	Bill
Halperin,	Jim	Snyder,	John
Hamilton,	Bruce	Spicer,	Bill
Haspel,	Mark	Steranko,	Jim
Hill,	Roger	Thomas,	Roy
Horvitz,	Tom	Thompson,	Maggie
Howard,	Bill	Vereneault,	Joe
Howell,	Rich	Weinberg,	Robert
Jaster,	Ed	White,	Greg
Kitchen,	Denis	Winiewicz,	Dave

ACTION COMICS No. 1

It was the middle of the Great Depression in America when two high school friends named Jerry Siegel and Joe Shuster began to develop their ideas for a new comic character they wanted to sell to the newspaper syndicates. Living in the midwest in Cleveland Ohio, these two young boys presented a precursor of their concept in a mimeographed science fiction fanzine (a self-published small press periodical) titled SCIENCE FICTION. Though "The Reign of the Superman" printed in the #3 (1933) issue of SCIENCE FICTION did not present this character as we know him today, the two young men were well on their way to introducing something totally new to the world.

Try and put yourself in their shoes for a moment. Let your imagination wander, and remember that in 1933-34 comic books had not begun their great run. The money and security, the exposure and fame, would come from placing a new comic character in the daily and Sunday newspaper comic sections. Popeye (for E.C. Segar), Tarzan (for Edgar Rice Burroughs), and Dick Tracy (for Chester Gould), had brought thousands of dollars in royalty payments for their creators and a lifetime of fame and popularity. In the middle of the Great Depression, this was the goal of our Cleveland team, to place Superman within the pages of the American newspapers.

Jerry Siegel was convinced that this new character, patterned after his favorite pulp characters Tarzan and John Carter of Mars would be a hit. He felt that if John Carter could leap over long distances from the lighter gravity of Mars, then his own new super character from another world would be able to leap over tall buildings with a single bound. Siegel figured quite correctly that if the public suspended disbelief for Buck Rogers and Flash Gordon, they would willingly embrace a "new" character like Superman.

However, the internal prejudice of the publishing business, and editors who thought that they were the experts on what young children wanted to read all led to a series of rejections for Siegel and Shuster and Superman. The young duo could not believe that every single newspaper syndicate that they presented their ideas to (with fully developed daily strips inked in and lettered professionally) would send the work back with comments like "too unbelievable," or "not within the realm of reality," or "its just too fantastic for readers to accept!" In a fit of depression, Joe Shuster destroyed these early works of art that would now be regarded as masterpieces and could sell for thousands of dollars in the collectors market!

But destiny would not be denied and after several more attempts at selling Superman to the newspaper syndicates and even Jerry Siegel's brief sojourn with another professional cartoonist to present his newfound concept, Superman as a character was sold. The sale was sudden and unexpected, and as so often happens in life, the process of birth would take many surprising turns.

As it turned out William M. Gaines (the father of E.C. comics publisher Bill Gaines), Sheldon Mayer (an editor for the McClure Syndicate in New York), and Harry Donnenfeld (co-owner of a printing plant which produced copies of DETECTIVE COMICS) would all collide and decide to take a chance on this new character named Superman. Without knowing exactly what impact their decision making process would produce, they decided to introduce (as the lead story) and feature on the cover this new character, in a brand new comic title called ACTION COMICS, which would sell for 10 cents.

Let your imagination wander again, back to the year 1939. Superman could not fly in the first several issues of ACTION COMICS. He was a slightly anarchistic character; he sometimes uttered thoughts like a socialist, not the flag-waving hero he would become during the years of World War II. He had a split personality, living by day as a drab newspaper reporter who couldn't impress his co-worker Lois Lane. Perhaps it was that important "Alter-ego" that gave the character some sense of mystery and let the imagination of young boys' soar through the air when he went into action and did his heroic deeds! Whatever it was, after the introductory issue of ACTION COMICS No. 1, the comic book industry was forever changed. A new era was about to be ushered in. All this change would come from the exploits of a single character, Superman. Just as Edgar Rice Burroughs' pulp character Tarzan had forever changed the face of pulp characters, so, too, would Clark Kent and Superman forever change the face of comic books.

Historical Value NEAR MINT- 9.2		
1970	1985	2004
$500	$15,000	$500,000

ACTION COMICS

10¢

FUNNIES ON PARADE

Ask science fiction and fantasy author Ray Bradbury what the first comics were and he will take you back to the Italian fresco paintings of Fra DeAngelico, or to earlier periods of time in human history. Ask most comic book fans what the first comic book was and they will split between two or three titles, but most will eventually settle on FUNNIES ON PARADE nn (no number), printed and distributed in 1933. This title belongs at the top of the list for most comic buffs because it really is the first four-color periodical to be published in a format similar to the comic books of today. It was printed ahead of *The Century of Comics*, and the popular *Famous Funnies: A Century of Comics*, which followed later in 1933.

However, this comic was not all in color for a dime. It was actually printed with the idea that it would be a promotional giveaway by the Proctor & Gamble Company. Anyone in 1933 interested in comics who came across this book could have it for free! The contents consisted of reprint Sunday comics sections for such popular characters as Bud Fisher's *Mutt & Jeff*, Ham Fisher's *Joe Palooka*, C. W. Kahle's *Hairbreadth Harry*, Gene Byrnes' *Regular Fellers*, Percy Crosby's *Skippy*, Frank Godwin's *Connie*, and *Keeping Up With The Jonseses*. This early comic was printed by the Eastern Printing Company and was the brainchild of Harry Wildenberg.

Harry Wildenberg's responsibility was to keep the presses running for Eastern Color at a point in time when business was in a slump. This same company printed some of the more popular Sunday color sections for newspaper syndicates, and because they ran large web plates for color, it was Wildenberg's job to keep these presses not only running but also using their full space capacity to print. Much of the same economics had earlier led the famous pulp publisher William Clayton to create ASTOUNDING STORIES in January of 1930 so that he could fill the final blank space left on his color cover run! They say that "necessity is the mother of invention," and just as William Clayton had looked to fill a hole, so, too, was Harry Wildenberg looking to run his presses at "full capacity." It's important to remember that Eastern had looked backward with the older fashioned stiff board covered premium comic "books" in mind when it issued this title, and it stayed with an already proven method of success, that of reprinting already popular newspaper comic characters familiar to the public at large. The cover brightly featured most of these characters on an attractive wrap-around design that was centered on the front by a big yellow ball with the title in red letters. Wildenberg, having previously experimented with promotional reprints for The Gulf Oil Company doing GULF COMIC WEEKLY, was all too ready to cooperate with the Proctor & Gamble Company when it placed an order for an astounding one million copies! This promotional give-away must have been tremendously successful in the spring of 1933, for at the same time, other publishers were looking at its format and asking the question: "Why couldn't we 'sell' this same package?"

It's also important to remember that the popularity and success of comic books share their evolution with another popular American readers' format publication, the paperback book. Both of these publishing ideas began with the idea that a publisher could "reprint" an already existing product, and reprint it in a very cheap fashion so that middle and lower middle class of America would have easy access to it. Not only could the publisher gain access to already existing content and pay a very small reprint fee, but also it could print it in a form cheap enough to allow them press runs in the thousands. This magic formula was perfect for the economic climate that was beginning to develop out of the depths of the 1930s depression. This approach fit in with movie theaters, radio shows that entertained hundreds of thousands of common people, Sunday afternoon picnics in the town squares, and other simple pleasures that were available to all people in all walks of life. But the comics, unlike the early paperback classic novels that were beginning to appear and the movies themselves, had a magic of their own. And they belonged to the children almost exclusively, or so it seemed at the beginning.

Historical Value NEAR MINT- 9.2		
1970	1985	2004
$125	$715	$17,000

FUNNIES ON PARADE

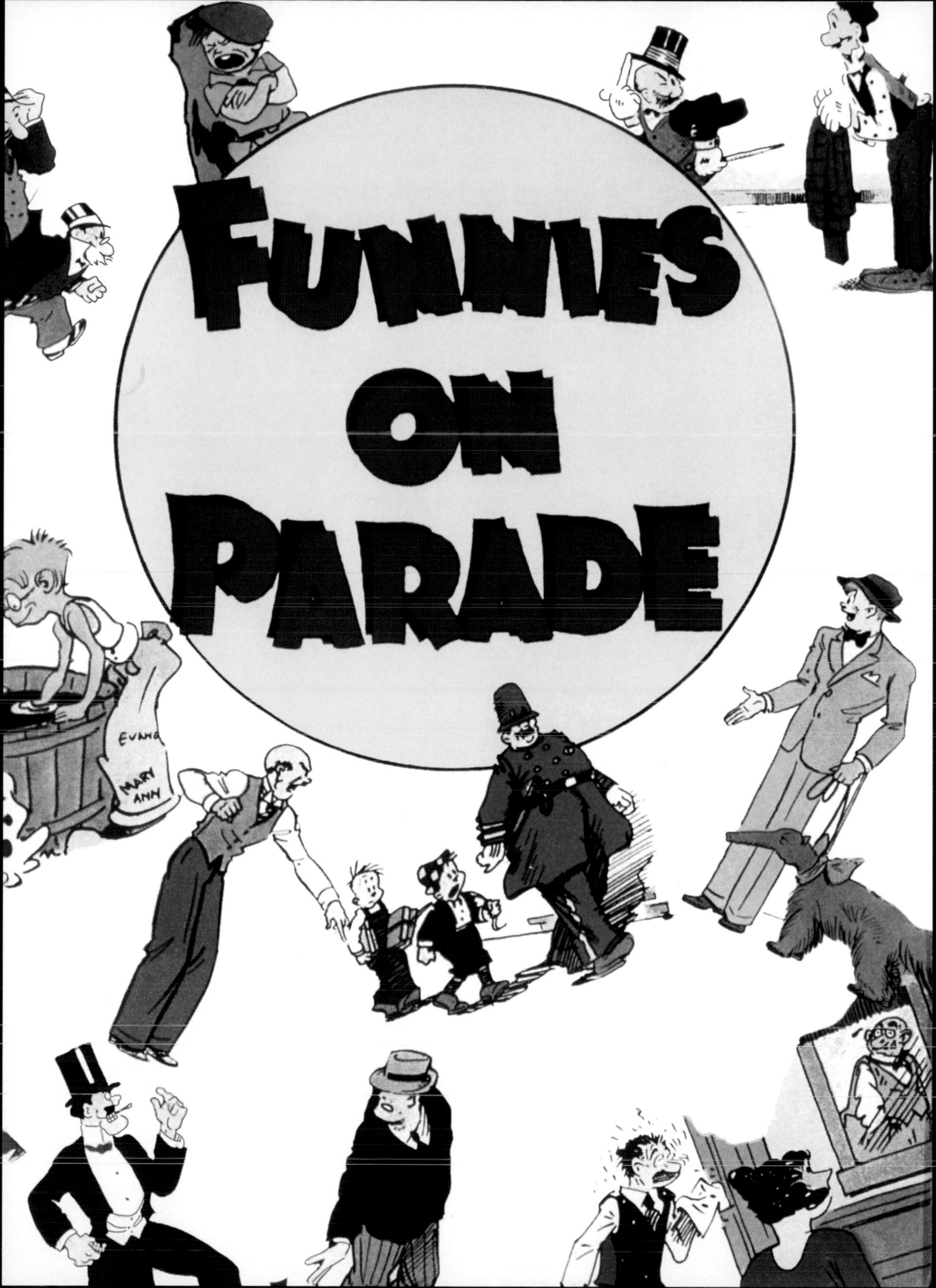

SUPERMAN No. 1

Of all the Golden Age superhero comic books, SUPERMAN No. 1 might perhaps be the "most saved" of them all. But a mystery persists to this day. Since so many were kept, why are there not any near perfect copies in existence today? If ever a comic book title helped to change the course of comics history, SUPERMAN No. 1 did not only that, but to this day helps explain precisely how the rare comic book market functions. Condition is King! This phrase in three words defines the entire comic book market. With the recent refinements to the grading standard and the advent of CGC, the comic containing and certified grading company, this mystery of condition vs. availability reminds all collectors that the common balance of "demand" vs. availability will continue to shape the course of markets for years to come.

SUPERMAN No. 1 primarily holds its important place in history because it was the first comic book title to feature the adventures of a single character created for the comics. After the popularity of Jerry Siegel and Joe Shuster's character in ACTION COMICS, it was decided by publisher DC Comics to give the character his own title. SUPERMAN No. 1 came out at the same time as the New York World's Fair of 1939, and it featured four reprinted stories from ACTION COMICS, along with a new two-page origin introduction, and a cover design based on a splash page from ACTION COMICS No. 10. The SUPERMAN title would quickly begin to feature all "original" stories and artwork with issues four through six.

The impact of this title on the newsstands was immediate, and it was not long before the Golden Age of Superhero comics would swing into full gear as publishers rushed to copy this successful format. But it was the original superhero character of Superman that would remain #1 with the kids of America from the beginning of the Golden Age until the also very popular and well-drawn character of Captain Marvel would overtake SUPERMAN in sales. Eventually, DC Comics would go to court against C.C. Beck's CAPTAIN MARVEL and Fawcett Publications, claiming that Fawcett had copied Superman. By the mid 1950s, DC would win a questionable lawsuit that would remove the red-clad competitor from the comic book market, until he re-appeared in the Bronze Age, ironically published by DC Comics!

SUPERMAN began to evolve with his own title; he would eventually fly, and other key characters in the plot were introduced such as arch villain Lex Luthor. It's interesting to note that the two most famous villains against both Batman and Superman did not make their appearances until each superhero was given his own title. Could this have been a search on the editor's part for more story plots and the desire for cliffhanger (taken from the movie serials) endings? We will never know, but an important component of the early Golden Age characters was that they were matched up against their colorful super-powered enemies. It was also during the first two years of the run that Superman began to take the turn toward being a more patriotic American hero as he began to battle the forces of evil in Germany and Japan. The covers for issues 12, 13, 14, 17, and 18 all featured Superman in some form of patriotic behavior.

But for all his popularity, and for all the saved copies, what about the "mystery" of why there are no perfect copies for SUPERMAN No. 1? ACTION COMICS No. 1, along with DETECTIVE COMICS No. 27 and MARVEL COMICS No. 1, all have examples of Very Fine to VF/NM copies known to survive. Some of the most famous examples come from the famed Edgar Church "Mile-High" Pedigree find (where there was one copy of nearly every single comic book from approximately 1939 to 1949 in near perfect condition), and other finds such as the Bethlehem Collection. For ACTION COMICS No. 1, at least four are known in Very Fine to better condition, as well as for DETECTIVE COMICS No. 27, with about six for MARVEL COMICS No. 1. Some people have suggested that SUPERMAN No. 1 was just "too" popular (and did not have the novelty that a first appearance might have provoked upon the part of an early buyer); therefore, the copies were read many times over. It doesn't hurt that the "Mile High" copy of SUPERMAN No. 1 was discovered flawed, or that the famed Bethlehem collection did not yield a high-grade copy of SUPERMAN No. 1. For whatever reason, if a Near Mint copy of SUPERMAN No. 1 were now to surface in the market place as an original discovery, and it was graded NM and confirmed as "not restored" by CGC, the public would be shocked with any results at auction. In this condition, the comic book might very well hammer at $250,000 or more!

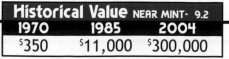

Historical Value	NEAR MINT- 9.2	
1970	1985	2004
$350	$11,000	$300,000

NEW FUN COMICS No. 1

NEW FUN COMICS No. 1 was exactly what the title implied when it came out in February of 1935. For the first time in America, a comic book was appearing with "original" stories and artwork. The fame and historical importance of this comic was first discussed by Coulton Waugh in his classic book *The Comics*, published by Luna Press in 1947. Waugh noted that, "Still another precedent was set early in 1935 by Major Malcolm Wheeler Nicholson, who came out with a four-color sixty-four-page magazine called NEW FUN. The Major had gone back to the 1929 idea of THE FUNNIES, for the contents of NEW FUN were original material. (It should be recorded here that original art-work had appeared in a one-color book called DETECTIVE DAN, in 1933). NEW FUN was shortly changed to MORE FUN, and Major Nicholson added another magazine, NEW ADVENTURE COMICS.

Malcolm W. Nicholson began his career in the comics business in 1934 when he began to develop his ideas about where the industry might be headed in the future. He had been in Europe and took note of how children's weekly cartoon papers were selling and he felt that the American market was ripe for new product. He had also observed that the European comic weeklies were full of mostly new material and did not rely upon reprints. Lloyd Jacquet would soon come in to team up with Nicholson and help him secure artists and writers who were willing to work for next to nothing. Their first real production would be a comic titled NEW FUN COMICS No. 1.

With NEW FUN, and NEW ADVENTURE, the Major had what would be the beginning of comics publishing giant DC, (National Periodical Publications) when Nicholson sold out to Harry Donnenfeld two years later. And although NEW FUN did have one other title (in the modern comic book format) before it in precedent with new material, the fact that it became one of the longest running comic titles during the 1930s through the 1940s assures its place in comics history. This first issue featured original stories that included the first appearance of Oswald The Rabbit, and a western feature entitled "Jack Woods" with artwork by L. Anderson. The price was 10 cents for this larger tabloid size comic book.

The impact upon the market place was not immediate, but the fact that this comic was printed and distributed had a profound impact on other publishers at the time. If these other publishers also knew that the Major was only paying a page rate of $5 each for a finished page, they might possibly have considered jumping on the "original" art band wagon quite some time sooner! Sadly, from the industry's very beginnings, a "cheap" price was set on the value of artistic and editorial labor by the publishers, and this trend would continue well into the 1960s. The impact of the depression most likely contributed to the ability of publishers to establish low page rates in the 1930s. However, given the real scarcity of jobs, for many young artists and writers, the opening market was an opportunity they could not wait to exploit for their own reasons. Will Eisner, Jack Kirby, Bill Everett, Lou Fine, Reed Crandall, Joe Shuster, Jerry Siegel, Carl Barks, Basil Wolverton, Jerry Robinson, Harry G. Peter, Bob Kane, Bernard Bailey, Jack Burnley, Walt Kelly, C. C. Beck, Alex Schomburg, and a host of other young men (and a few women) were just beginning to consider a career in comics; they were about to forever change the face of popular culture in America! And all this from an industry that would sell the product for 10 cents, and pay for editorial and artistic output at the lowest possible rates!

Because this particular title was printed and bound in a large format its scarcity in high-grade is remarkable. The *Overstreet Comic Price Guide* has for years carried no listing above Very Fine, and this book is now valued at over $40,000 in the Very Fine category. There are no true Mint copies known to exist, and the famed "Mile High" Pedigree Collection did not yield a copy of the first issue of NEW FUN COMICS No. 1. For collectors of this early title, just having a Good + example would be the norm.

NEW FUN COMICS No. 1 could therefore be considered one of the truly RARE examples of early comic books with very few high-grade copies known to exist. Possibly fewer than five copies are known in above "unrestored" FINE condition. The fact that this comic book is now also considered the first DC comic title also adds to its importance and desirability for collectors. As time goes by, its real place in comic history will be confirmed, and the ability of collectors to find copies in any condition at all will continue to push the price ever upward.

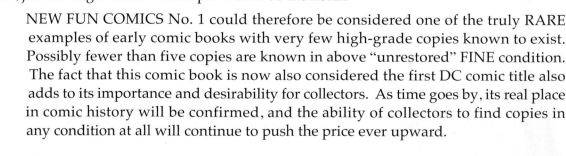

Historical Value	NEAR MINT- 9.2	
1970	1985	2004
$100	$1,200	$55,000

NEW FUN COMICS No. 1

MAD No. 1

Bill Gaines used to say repeatedly to his friends that the birth of MAD came from the simple fact that Harvey Kurtzman had pushed himself into exhaustion and a severe case of yellow jaundice during the summer of 1952. Kurtzman had come to EC Comics during the early part of 1950 and was immediately given story assignments for the early issues of the horror and science fiction titles. He enjoyed this work at the beginning, but then began to chafe at the limitations of these two genres. Eventually, as EC expanded and became more successful, Gaines gave Kurtzman what he really wanted, the editorial control over two new EC titles: TWO-FISTED TALES and later FRONTLINE COMBAT.

Kurtzman would eventually become so dedicated to producing historically correct and realistic comic book narratives that he would drive himself into exhaustion and his artists into states of nearly violent "war-like" behavior! When Harvey became sick during the summer of 1952 and was at the same time asking for a pay raise from EC, Bill Gaines hit upon the idea of giving him another new title. Gaines suggested to Kurtzman that he do a "humorous" comic book title. Gaines was well aware of Kurtzman's previous artistic efforts for Stan Lee at Marvel Comics for HEY LOOK, and he had seen panels for GENIUS and SILVER LININGS, so it seemed like a perfect idea to encourage Kurtzman to do a humorous magazine for EC.

MAD No. 1 was released in October/November of 1952 and had much of the same impact that ACTION COMICS No. 1 did when it came out. However, this revolution was at first a very quiet one. Other publishers did rush in with a few copy-cat titles (and EC would shortly create its own "copy" title PANIC, edited by Al Feldstein), but there was no real physical evidence that something "new" had come into the marketplace that would change it forever. But that's just what happened. People as diverse as Robert Crumb (who stated that his eyeballs fell out of his head when he picked up the first issue of MAD), Denis Kitchen (who would go on to found Kitchen Sink Press), Frank Zappa (who would later take out ads for his Mothers of Invention records in comic books), and Harlan Ellison (who would just as dramatically change the course of science fiction during the 1950s and 1960s), and a host of others declared MAD a breath of fresh creative air the likes of which America had never before seen.

MAD poked fun at virtually every aspect of America. Popular music, the advertising field, television and radio, social habits like dating, politics, and, yes, even the comics themselves were the target of Kurtzman's humor. And while the artists of the EC staff were sometimes previously at odds with Kurtzman's neurotic and controlling behavior (he would design out panel by panel progressions for each page, with drawn in panels for the artists to follow!) over at TWO-FISTED TALES, they burst forth with a string of MADnificent illustrations for their MAD stories! Comic readers everywhere couldn't wait for the latest issue of MAD so they could see what the feverish editor and his artists had come up with next, and they were rarely disappointed! Somehow in the middle of the staid 1950s, right before the McCarthy period was about to reach the top of its abuse, and at a time in American culture when few were willing to take chances, MAD came into its own.

A short discussion about why MAD No. 1 has the most Near Mint copies in existence among the top ten comics is both interesting and revealing to readers not familiar with comics history. Bill Gaines, the publisher of EC Comics and MAD, was one of the most unusual characters ever to enter the comics industry. His almost prophetic ability to see where the comics market was headed in the early 1950s was matched by his profound (and almost single-handed) decision to store and keep every single page of artwork to every story and cover for every EC comic book. His artists and editors used to scream, "Bill you're crazy, what will you ever do with it all?" And Bill would scream back: "I'll sell it later for thousands of dollars, and have last laugh on the lot of you!" Not only did publisher Gaines save the artwork, but also he had assistant Jerry DeFuccio meticulously pull and store twelve (or up to twelve) copies of every single comic book that he published!

Can anyone imagine the impact if DC Comics had done the same thing at its offices starting in 1939? Well, Gaines had the last laugh on all fronts - with MAD, with his original EC artwork (a percentage of the profits which he shared with all living EC artists when it was sold by Russ Cochran during the 1970s), and then eventually with the Gaines File copies, which are now CGC-contained and sell for thousands of dollars each. And the Gaines File copies for MAD No. 1? Hoo-Haa! - You should be so lucky to own one of these ferslussiner books! You'll go MAD trying to obtain one today!

Historical Value NEAR MINT- 9.2		
1970	1985	2004
$30	$400	$14,000

MAD No.1

TALES CALCULATED TO DRIVE YOU
MAD
HUMOR IN A JUGULAR VEIN
AN ENTERTAINING EC COMIC
No.1
OCT.-NOV.
10¢
THAT THING! THAT SLITHERING BLOB COMING TOWARD US!
WHAT IS IT?
IT'S MELVIN!

MICKEY MOUSE MAGAZINE No. 1 (1933)

Reflecting on the early days, Disney never heard of a comic book in 1932 because such a thing didn't exist. There were only newspapers, books and magazines. A lot of comic material had been published, much reprinted and some original, but always in a book or magazine format. Much research has been done on the Platinum Age and its significance is just now beginning to become clear. The action of folding a sheet of paper of an established size and trimming it out to 64 pages and then adding a cover was an accident of timing and need, not particularly brilliant in concept. At this time Kay Kamen at Disney – the merchandising guru – had the green light from Walt to develop things to sell. Disney had already started licensing books, but the problem was people would buy one and that was it. Kamen realized he wanted continuity and only a comic magazine could do that, published monthly. But he had a problem. Would parents buy one for their kids? Wouldn't it be better to reach the kids themselves? Where were they when they were most susceptible? At the movies where they'd just seen Mickey Mouse! But they would have to be cheap, something kids could afford. How about a nickel comic book magazine sold in the theatres along with popcorn and candy? It would have to be small, and maybe with only one color besides black. MICKEY MOUSE MAGAZINE No. 1 thus appeared in January 1933 and this one small step launched a chain reaction that would affect the Disney Empire forever!

Kamen soon learned the problem was the theatres. They'd rather sell popcorn for more profit and less fuss. Within nine months he was back at the drawing board with the idea to sell this same product to dairies with individualized advertising printed for each dairy on the cover. From dairies to kids was Kamen's intent. So he started the same book over again, and not wanting to own up to his previous nine month failure started the numbering over again with No. 1! This time Disney had more success, for two years and twenty four issues. However comparing the relative success of this Dairy campaign to the apparent sales of comic strip books now on the newsstands, Disney decided to leap into the market with another MICKEY MOUSE MAGAZINE. Disney figured if we can't give away small comic magazines this time we'll go BIG! So, for a third time with no break in publishing continuity, Kamen started over in 1935 with his giant-size MICKEY MOUSE MAGAZINE No. 1 in full color, expanding the comics and the stories but keeping the same general format idea and painted covers. However, because of the size and costs of printing (they were expensive to produce) Kamen soon adjusted the size and comic strips were inserted with more regularity to save on budget costs.

After MICKEY MOUSE MAGAZINE was discontinued, the Walt Disney Company actually continued paid subscriptions with a lead in to WALT DISNEY'S COMICS & STORIES. They did this without missing a month in continuity and without changing a thing in the format. This continuity that began the run in 1935 lasting to this day qualifies as the longest running continuity in comic book history. Considering that this would also include the best selling title, the MICKEY MOUSE MAGAZINE ranks as one of the most important comics ever published for the entire industry.

THE 100 GREATEST COMIC BOOKS

Historical Value	NEAR MINT- 9.2	
1970	1985	2004
$125	$600	$17,500

MICKEY MOUSE MAGAZINE No. 1

ZAP COMICS No. 1

When a lanky dark-haired shy young man began to appear on the streets of Haight Ashbury in San Francisco during the fall of 1967, just after the famous "summer of love," panhandling his "homemade" comic book, few people realized that another turning point in the history of comics was about to happen. Crumb's ZAP COMICS was preceded by many ground-breaking examples (such as GOD NOSE by Jack Jackson hailing from Austin Texas in 1964; S. Clay Wilson's loose leaf port-folio of TWENTY DRAWINGS finished in the summer of 1967; and Joel Beck's legendary green cover LENNY OF LAREDO from 1965); however, it would be ZAP COMICS No. 1 that became the rallying point and focus of the next big change in the history of comics.

The first edition of ZAP COMICS No.1 was printed by a local hipster and poet. In thin blue letters on the back cover, this important first printing is noted as "Printed by Charles Plymell." Among other characteristics, such as overlapping untrimmed pages, the 25-cent cover price (all in black and white for two dimes and a nickel!), and a light yellow cover color (instead of the orange color used on the Don Donahue 2nd printing), this first issue contained content decidedly different from most comic books that came before. As a teenager, Crumb had been inspired by Harvey Kurtzman's MAD, and he would continue to develop and expand ideas introduced by Kurtzman's satire with ZAP COMICS.

By the second issue, Crumb was opening the doors of this title to other interested artists and the famous "jam combina-tion" of S. Clay Wilson, Rick Griffin, Robert Williams, Spain Rodriguez, Victor Moscoso, and Gilbert Shelton would lend their talents to each succeeding issue. The artists were free from any constraint of content to do whatever they wished, and they began to rotate the cover assignments for each issue and include one "jam" page as well. After the first few printings of the early issues, The Print Mint owned by Bob Rita took over the chores of printing and distribution. By 1969 the counter-culture was in full bloom, and "underground comix," as they had come to be known, were appearing all over the country.

ZAP COMICS remained in the vanguard of this movement due to the talent of the original "seven" artists who kept it going. In each issue, readers were confronted with unprecedented stories such as S. Clay Wilson's masterpiece of Beat/Surrealist/Fantasy entitled "Star-Eyed Stella," or Spain's incredible "Field Meet," where the Road Vultures and the Sparrows (different Biker clubs) encountered each other in an afternoon of spiritual discourse! The oldest artist, Victor Moscoso, was a professor of print making at the San Francisco Institute of Art, and he encouraged each artist to copyright each story in his name, control the future royalties, and in general, sign deals with publisher Bob Rita that would protect their rights as artists. This small act by an individual team would soon have a profound effect upon the entire mainstream comics industry as other artists working for Marvel and DC soon found out that the artists doing the Underground Comics owned all the rights, artwork, and future royalties to their own characters! It would not be long before Neal Adams and other professional comics artists would begin to pressure both DC and Marvel for the return of all their original artwork and better publishing terms. The Underground Comix also defied the Comics Code Authority and brought about a completely new system of distribution for comics. These examples would soon be followed by mainstream publishers and the remark-able efforts of Brooklyn resident Phil Seuling, who would soon start up the "Direct Market" distribution system that would completely re-invent the way mainstream comics books were distributed.

The changes wrought by ZAP were enormous. Crumb and his band of creative pranksters had brought about a total redefinition of what it was to draw and publish comic books. Not only did ZAP challenge the content and self-censorship that comics had been living under since the demise of TALES FROM THE CRYPT, its example caused changes to ripple out into the American culture at large. Harvey Kurtzman, when working for Playboy magazine and years removed from MAD, could only look upon all these changes with satisfaction. The right of the individual artist to own his product, including the original artwork after its being printed, the ability of authors and artists to cut independent movie deals or commercial applications of their characters, the ability of publishers to distribute more directly to their buying public, all of this came from the example of ZAP COMICS. After Crumb had shown them the way, could the explosive talents and creations of Neil Gaiman, Alan Moore, Dave Gibbons, or Frank Miller be far behind?

Historical Value NEAR MINT- 9.2		
1970	1985	2004
$25	$250	$4,000

MARVEL COMICS No. 1

MARVEL COMICS No. 1 stands out from the crowd of premier Golden Age comic books for a number of reasons. Its place in history is secure (despite whatever arguments remain regarding with MARVEL No. 1 vs. MOTION PICTURE FUNNIES No. 1 hosting the appearance of the Everett Sub-Mariner story). MARVEL No. 1 introduced the standard Golden Age characters of The Human Torch by Carl Burgos, The Sub-Mariner by Bill Everett, The Angel by Paul Gustavson, and Ka-zar the Great by Ben Thompson. MARVEL COMICS No. 1 also hosts the only painted cover for a first issue Golden Age title. The painting was by science fiction's master of the genre, Frank R. Paul. Paul was famous for doing 99% of the covers of Hugo Gernsback's AMAZING STORIES, all of the covers for SCIENCE WONDER STORIES, SCIENCE WONDER QUARTERLY, and later WONDER STORIES. This powerful painting of the Human Torch blazing through a wall to confront a man with a gun was chosen over an equally interesting painted concept by Bill Everett depicting The Sub-Mariner rising out of a burst of water. Timely comics titles would become the great alternative to DC Comics, and along with Fawcett Publications would provide the most serious competition during the Golden Age of comics to the otherwise overwhelming popularity of the DC titles. This early first issue also has two variants of its front cover because it was originally dated for release in October 1939. Because it was released late, most numbers have a "black" circular stamp over the front cover date and on the inside a small square rectangle stamp with "November" printed over it. Can anyone imagine a modern publication anywhere today where the entire print run had these kinds of hand corrections? The entire print run didn't get all of the corrections; some copies got out without the stamping and are considered the more "scarce" and desirable to the two variants. Not only did Timely have trouble with the dates, but the interior pages for this important comic are famous for having off-registration printing. This off-registration printing happened with the highest number of copies right in the middle of Bill Everett's classic origin story for The Sub-Mariner. But despite all of these "differences," high-grade copies of MARVEL COMICS No. 1 are evaluated by their physical structure, and they are not downgraded by having off-registered interior pages.

The Timely (later, Marvel) characters were immediately recognized as being "different" from the DC line of superheroes. Sub-Mariner was an "anti-hero," and from issue to issue readers could not figure whether he was a superhero or super-villain. The Human Torch was a dangerous freak of nature as the result of a laboratory experiment gone wrong. Eventually, Timely would introduce CAPTAIN AMERICA, a more traditional patriotic character. However, the Alex Schomburg and Jack Kirby/Joe Simon covers for CAPTAIN AMERICA would become so off-beat, full of "bondage" and violent themes that comic readers still considered Timely colorful to say the least.

Surviving copies of MARVEL COMICS No. 1 in middle grades are more common than copies of ACTION COMICS No.1 or DETECTIVE COMICS No. 27. For years during the 1970s and '80s, MARVEL No. 1's sold for less than ACTION COMICS No. 1. Part of the reason for this might be that there were too many copies available, or that for some mysterious reason there were large numbers in near Fine available in the market. More adults may have bought and saved MARVEL COMICS No. 1 because it had a painted (and therefore more adult) cover. We will never know for sure. Perhaps the most famous surviving copy of MARVEL COMICS No. 1 is the "Pay-Out" Timely file copy, which was offered for sale at Sotheby's 1993 June 26th sale. This extremely high-grade copy (it was graded by Sotheby's AACBC grading committee at Very Fine –89,) failed to meet its reserve price of $60,000 at the time but has since sold for a whopping $350,000! The "Pay-Out" copy has pencil notations on the cover and interior pages stating what each artist was paid for each story, so not only is this copy desirable for its overall high-grade, but also is a rare historical example of how the comic book market functioned in its beginning years. In 2002 a high-grade copy of the Denver MARVEL COMICS No. 1 sold for an astonishing $250,000! It would seem that the times have caught up with this important title, and no one is complaining anymore about its inability to sell at high prices!

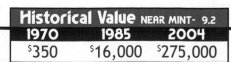

Historical Value NEAR MINT- 9.2		
1970	1985	2004
$350	$16,000	$275,000

MARVEL COMICS No. 1

WHIZ COMICS No. 2   (No. 1)

WHIZ COMICS No. 2 is probably the most publicly forgotten important early title of the Golden Age of comics. Why this is so, and the history behind how Captain Marvel gave Superman such a run for his money and then eventually overtook the Man of Steel in newsstand sales, is important to understanding the early superhero comics of the 1940s. As original as Superman was, even with his alter-ego Clark Kent, his surrounding staff at the Daily Planet, and his cast of super villains, he was almost no match in the end for the genius of C.C. Beck's Captain Marvel character. For the alter-ego of Captain Marvel was none other than a small boy named Billy Batson who could become Captain Marvel by uttering the magic words S-H-A-Z-A-M!

The "S" stood for Solomon (wisdom); the "H" for Hercules (strength); the "A" for Atlas (stamina); the "Z" for Zeus (power); the "A" for Achilles (courage); and the "M" for Mercury (speed). When C. C. Beck first started work for Fawcett Publications in the fall of 1939, he was assigned one of three new characters invented for Fawcett by staff writer Bill Parker. Beck's inking style was perfect for Captain Marvel: he had a strong linear design for his figures; his backgrounds were simple but solid, and his ability to grasp and illustrate the story plots were full of imaginative visual surprises. But where Fawcett was ahead of the rest of the pack with Beck as artist they also had some of the leading pulp Science fiction writers of the time scripting the stories for Captain Marvel. The likes of Manly Wade Wellman, Joseph Millard, Bill Woolfolk, and Otto Binder turned in finished scripts for Captain Marvel in the 1940s.

The alter-ego of any superhero during the 1940s usually gravitated between the "mild-mannered" Joe next door–or, a "vulnerable" character–and that of the super-powered invulnerable hero who could rarely be stopped or harmed. Why this appealed to young readers is self-evident and its origins in literature go back at least to Homer and the Greek gods. How could Clark Kent really compete with the younger Billy Batson? Billy was constantly getting himself into trouble (just like any small child), and his adventures revolved around the super-powered Captain Marvel coming into being to right the problem. But Billy seemed "real" to his readers; in fact, he was the true proto-type for Peter Parker, the mild-mannered teenager who would appear years later in comics as Spider-Man and re-define the entire concept of an alter ego!

As the Big Red Cheese (as Captain Marvel came to be known) began to overtake Superman in sales, there was a short-lived attempt by the editorial staff at Fawcett to get rid of the alter-ego personification of Billy Batson. Fortunately, this idea never came to pass. There were also complaints from the editorial offices that Beck imbued his super-villains with too much of a sympathetic viewpoint and aura; they were almost likable! Again, Beck was working on instinct, and without question, the younger readers related to Captain Marvel because he was their own fantasy of the kind of superhero they would like to become, and they most likely were entertained by super-villains who were not too dark or scary. Sivana (a classic mad scientist in the Frankenstein tradition), Mr. Mind (who was nothing more than an intelligent worm!), Ibac, Oggar, and King Kull all brought great confrontations to Captain Marvel in their adventures.

DC Comics, after pursuing a lawsuit in court against Fawcett and Captain Marvel for years, finally got the judgment that it was after all along in the 1950s. DC maintained that Captain Marvel was a copy of Superman and incredibly, after the age of superheroes was over and done with, a court of law judged in favor of the DC complaint! After winning the fight on the newsstands fair and square, the Big Red Cheese was retired from the pages of comics until DC later revived him under its own banner in the 1970s as "Shazam."

The comics would never be the same. Dick Lupoff's famous science fiction fanzine XERO gave credit to the Fawcett Comics line in the No.1 issue in 1960, when Lupoff wrote the first in a continuing series of articles entitled "All In Color For a Dime;" his first installment was "The Big Red Cheese." Less than two years later in 1962, with XERO No. 9, Roy Thomas would continue with his precise "Captain Billy's Whiz Gang." This fifteen-page article (with illustrations), along with Lupoff's, was the beginning of fandom's revival of interest in the Golden Age character that would over time be relegated to a position considerably behind Superman, but who would remain first forever in the hearts and minds of those who came of age during the heyday of Captain Marvel.

Historical Value NEAR MINT- 9.2		
1970	1985	2004
$250	$8,000	$75,000

WHIZ COMICS No. 2 (No. 1)

BATMAN No. 1

There are probably more copies of BATMAN No. 1 surviving today than any of the other top six titles; and part of the reason might be its tremendous front cover design. Batman creator Bob Kane was still doing the artwork at the time this premiere issue appeared, and his photograph is featured (with him at his drawing board) inside with a special spotlight on the artist. The number one issue is composed almost entirely of stories originally scheduled for DETECTIVE COMICS and, because of this, the first issue has the first appearance of The Joker, the first appearance of female villain Catwoman, and the first pin-up design on a back cover. This comic hit the newsstands in the spring of 1940.

With so many changes in the character over the years, it's easy to forget that this comic book superhero was the perfect blend of previous pulp characters and the more modern idea of a costumed hero. THE SHADOW had been running successfully in the pulp magazines since the spring of 1931. In addition, the early superhero character Doc Savage also enjoyed a long run in the pulps and detective pulp titles were rampant during the 1930s. Batman was the perfect combination of some of these previous characters and he relied primarily on his skills as a detective, unlike Superman and other heroes who carried the day with their super-powers. Artist and creator Bob Kane was well aware of what had come before, and when he was approached by DC Comics to develop a character for its title DETECTIVE COMICS, he felt compelled to create a character that used the night and the shadow-land of men's fears to combat the world of crime.

By 1940, superhero titles were just beginning to flood the newsstands, and Batman was now appearing in DETECTIVE COMICS, his own title BATMAN, and teamed up with Superman in WORLD'S FINEST COMICS, and appeared on a regular basis with Robin the Boy Wonder in STAR SPANGLED COMICS. But it was the atmospheric quality of the early Bob Kane style that originally propelled this character to stardom status. Kane drew in a wooden style where the characters, who always seemed frozen in-between "action" movements, and the background castles, dark Manhattan-style Gotham City street scenes, and ghoulish villains (right out of the pages of pulp magazines) were both original and foreboding in their appearance. No other comic book character except The Spectre and The Shadow (when he jumped into comics in March of 1940) could portray the "dark" side of life quite so effectively, which may be why the Batman has been brought back to his pulp roots many times over in the 1960s (by Neal Adams), and again in the 1980s (by Frank Miller) and beyond by a host of newer artists and writers.

Historical Value NEAR MINT- 9.2		
1970	1985	2004
$175	$5,000	$125,000

BATMAN No. 1

WALT DISNEY'S COMICS & STORIES No. 1

Looking back, it would seem inevitable that the Walt Disney Company would eventually enter into the comics publishing craze of the 1940s, how could it resist? Disney characters were without question famous, recognized worldwide, and popular by the time that four-color comics became a hit on the newsstands at 10 cents each. All Disney had to do was license, and license it did! The Whitman Publishing Company had already flooded the market with attractive Disney cardboard cover books, Big Little Books, and early comic proto-type periodicals during the early 1930s, and now that comic books were in vogue, they began to make their move.

WALT DISNEY'S COMICS & STORIES No. 1 appeared in October 1940. This comic came from the earlier successful MICKEY MOUSE MAGAZINE, which ran in a larger magazine size format, with mixed black and white and color interior artwork and stories. The cover for the first issue of WALT DISNEY'S COMICS & STORIES featured Donald Duck. The interior stories for Donald Duck in this issue were illustrated by Al Taliaferro (who did the newspaper daily and Sunday Donald Duck sections), and Floyd Gottfredson (who also did the daily and Sunday newspaper comic sections for Mickey Mouse), and were published by Dell Comics. The early issues of W.D.C. & S. carried reprint strips for Donald Duck and Mickey Mouse, and then with later issues original material began to appear.

W.D.C.& S. is recognized as the first Funny Animal comic book within a running series. It would eventually become the largest selling comic in America under the stewardship of Carl Barks, who beginning with issue No. 31, turned the Donald Duck stories into classics of everyday life. Donald Duck was a character everyone could sympathize with. Donald constantly lost his temper, he played the fool to a number of situations in life both domestically and socially, he was the guardian of three small boys, he could never seem to hold down a job for long, and he was certainly middle class in both

his aspirations and education. Mickey Mouse already had his popularity confirmed from the animated movies, and his cartoon character never really developed beyond the standard persona introduced in the 1930s, excepting the excellent work of Floyd Gottfredson in newspaper strips. It took the comic book format for Donald to flower, and bloom he did!

WALT DISNEY'S COMICS & STORIES would also feature cover artwork by Walt Kelly, it would introduce a number of new characters including Uncle Scrooge (in issue No. 98 for November 1948), and it would continue well into the 1970s and 1980s without interruption. The publishing progression moved from Dell to Gold Key (in the 1960s), to Whitman, and eventually to Gladstone Comics in the 1990s where a series of loving reprints brought all the Disney characters back to life. Disney has now licensed to Diamond Comics, and from the Gladstone editions to the newer comics, younger readers are being introduced to the joys of reading a Carl Barks' story.

Historical Value NEAR MINT- 9.2		
1970	1985	2004
$115	$3,000	$30,000

AMAZING FANTASY No. 15

For sheer impact, and as a symbol of the singular change that the Silver Age wrought, AMAZING FANTASY No. 15 (August 1962) should stand shoulder to shoulder with ACTION COMICS No. 1. Superhero comic themes had been around for twenty four years without any cessation of publication (honoring the DC six which survived the middle 1950s), when Stan Lee came up with the idea for a new superhero which he quickly assigned to Marvel staff artist Steve Ditko to illustrate. No one could have realized that a completely new era was about to be defined and galvanized by a superhero concept that at first seemed absurd and ridiculous! The Spider-Man had appeared in AMAZING FANTASY No. 15 because the owner of Marvel Comics, Martin Goodman, was not keen on the concept, and had given Lee the use of a throw away title that was about to be cancelled.

But a new idea was indeed afoot, and as Bob Dylan was just about to sing, "The times they were a changin'!" To begin with, the alter-ego for this new character was a thin, timid, withdrawn, an unpopular loser (kind of a Charlie Brown of the high school set) who was not only bookish, but also incredibly inept with girls, and doted upon his Aunt May and Uncle Ben. However, due to a twist of fate, and the bite of a radioactive spider, this young man was soon to become the amazing Spider-Man. Somehow it seemed that fate had not only delivered Peter Parker to that spider – but also Steve Ditko to Stan Lee, for never before had an artist been born to the task of illustrating a comic character as Ditko was for Spider-Man. Apparently, the assignment for Spider-Man was originally given to Jack Kirby, but Lee did not like the "muscleman" approach and switched to the "suit" style of Ditko who changed the look and costume to the published form.

Ditko had an uncanny inking style somewhat akin to the earlier science fiction illustrator Edd Cartier (where faces, old, young, ugly, and beautiful, were drenched with individual characteristics and expressions), and his ability to infuse his characters within the small space of each panel with real life emotions made the progressive story lines for Spider-Man extra special for readers. SPIDER-MAN became the choice of the more "hip" comic book readers who were drawn into the comic fold to follow Ditko's artwork and Lee's writing.

A curious anomaly with the production of early Marvel titles has resulted in very few surviving Near Mint or Mint copies for this important comic book. Marvel was just about bankrupt when Spider-Man and the Silver Age burst upon the scene in 1962; its paper cover stock was so thin that when the printers would stack the bundles up for trimming–no matter how sharp the cutting edge of the blade–some small nicks and parts of the right hand cover would come off. This came to be known as a "Marvel Edge," and about 85% of all AMAZING FANTASY No. 15's have some evidence of this flaw in their covers. The irony? As few near perfect copies as there are of ACTION COMICS No. 1, there are almost just as few near perfect copies of AMAZING FANTASY No. 15!

Historical Value NEAR MINT- 9.2		
1970	1985	2004
$30	$2,000	$60,000

If Fawcett Publications correctly understood the obvious connection between its audience of children and the superhero concept, it would seem as if the rest of the comics publishing world was asleep at the wheel for about two months! Fawcett had accomplished the obvious when it created the "young" boy Billy Batson to become the alter-ego of Captain Marvel. By having a boy as the alter-ego of a superhero, Fawcett leapt over DC's Clark Kent (who was a mild mannered reporter, but an adult!), and made the DIRECT connection between the adult and powerful hero, and the younger and inexperienced reader, the child. After waiting for nearly two years, the public finally picked up DETECTIVE COMICS No. 38 in April 1940 to find a colorful cover depicting a young costumed character bursting through a circular papered circus ring held by Batman. Robin the Boy Wonder was being introduced!

DETECTIVE COMICS No. 38 was the first superhero comic book to introduce the concept of the junior side-kick. Within months, other companies followed suit. Captain America had Bucky, Sandman had Sandy, Catwoman had the Kitten, Mr. Scarlet had Pinky, along with a host of other junior characters. DETECTIVE No. 38 probably also brought about other title changes including CAPTAIN MARVEL JR. published in November 1942, and the appearance of Kid Eternity in HIT COMICS No. 25 for December 1942.

What Robin brought to the table was every young reader's fantasy. The kids pictured themselves doing great acts of daring and heroism, and buried within their hearts, they secretly wanted to join their favorite comic characters in each story. Now they had a character with whom to identify! DC may have picked Batman as the perfect candidate because unlike Superman (who already had a great surrounding cast of characters at the *Daily Planet* with Lois Lane, Jimmy Olsen, a sort of annoying junior side kick to Clark Kent, and his editor Perry White), Bruce Wayne was a withdrawn man who, excepting his trusted butler Alfred, avoided social entanglements.

Robin would become so popular later in the 1940s that for a short period of time he would be featured exclusively on the covers and interior stories of STAR SPANGLED COMICS from issue 65 through 95, and then with interior stories only up to issue No. 130. Like Batman, his young ward Dick Grayson also experienced personal hardships in his life from the effects of crime. Both Bruce Wayne's and Robin's parents were murdered in front of their eyes. Both shared the bond of having dedicated their lives to fighting crime. Comics, and especially superhero comics, would never be the same after Robin's DETECTIVE COMICS No. 38 introduction.

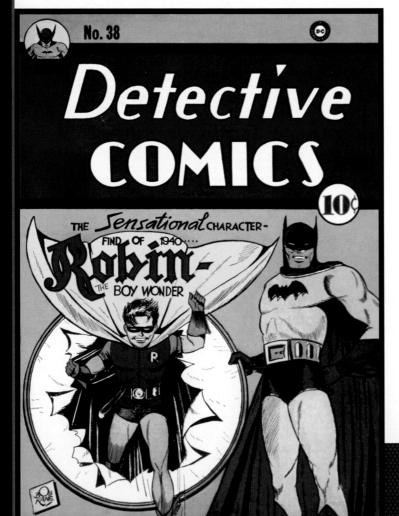

Historical Value NEAR MINT- 9.2		
1970	1985	2004
$60	$1,800	$55,000

ALL STAR COMICS was originally conceived by DC Comics as a showcase title for some of its secondary characters in the summer of 1940 when it was circulated to newsstands. Within two issues, however, DC made a startling change, and instead of featuring each of its characters in an individual story within the comic title, it introduced them on the cover of the No. 3 Winter 1940 issue as the "Justice Society of America!" Thus was born the first comic book with a superhero team, brought together and dedicated to fighting evil and crime wherever it may appear.

The Justice Society was the brainchild of one or more of the following individuals: Sheldon Mayer, who was an editor at DC during 1940, Max Gaines, the co-publisher and managing editor for DC, Garder F. Fox who was a writer at this time, and publisher Harry Donnenfeld who would have had to approve of the idea once it came from the others. The early issues of ALL STAR were plotted and written by Mayer and Fox. Later, the progression of editors for these stories was Whitney Ellsworth, Ted Udall, Dorothy Robicek, and eventually Julius Schwartz and Robert Kanigher. Schwartz would become a fan favorite, and because he stayed with DC during the dark years (at least for superhero costumed characters) of 1950 through 1956, he would be in a remarkable position to revive the superheroes, begin the Silver Age of comics, and include in it a new version of the Justice Society entitled "The Justice League of America."

The cover for ALL STAR COMICS No. 3 featured (left to right) The Atom, Sandman, The Spectre, The Flash, Hawkman, Dr. Fate, Green Lantern, and The Hourman (Johnny Thunder was not pictured) all sitting at a round table with the large letters blazing across the surface "JUSTICE SOCIETY of AMERICA." The design logo below this illustration featured the name of each hero and the statement, "in brand new episodes as personally related at the first meeting of the Justice Society of America." Issue No. 4 featured the first combined adventure story where every character appeared at once, and thereafter a series of classic and beautifully designed covers developed this powerful new idea of the super-team in comics.

When organized comics fandom began to develop in the early 1960s, ALL STAR COMICS were some of the most favorite and nostalgically remembered of all the Golden Age comics. Roy Thomas was a huge ALL STAR fan, and this author owned beautiful high-grade copies of ALL STAR #'s 4, 5, 6, 7, 8, 9, 12-22 and others (the rare No. 3 was never obtained!) – they were among some of his most prized comic books. Why this comic title remained so popular long after its demise can be explained in part by the fact that history had caught up with the original idea. When the Silver Age of comics burst forth in the 1960s, comics like THE AVENGERS, THE X-MEN, THE DOOM PATROL, THE FANTASTIC FOUR, and THE JUSTICE LEAGUE OF AMERICA all confirmed that the superhero team up was an idea set into the firmament of comics mythology.

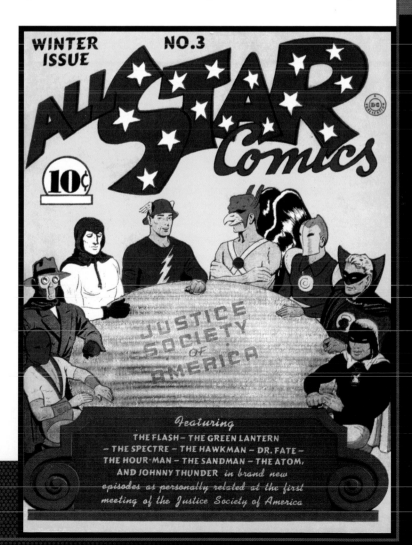

Historical Value NEAR MINT- 9.2		
1970	1985	2004
$135	$2,250	$75,000

CAPTAIN AMERICA COMICS No. 1

The front cover for CAPTAIN AMERICA COMICS No. 1 pretty much said it all when the March 1941 issue was released. The artwork for this dramatic cover was done by Jack Kirby and Syd Shores, with interior artwork by Jack Kirby and Joe Simon. The front cover featured a top logo with red, white and blue stripes, the figure of Captain America (using a shield shaped in the form of a "V" soon to be changed to a circle), landing a hard right-handed fist to the jaw of Adolf Hitler, while armed Nazi guards fired upon him from all directions. Captain America's young side-kick Bucky was featured in a circle at the bottom of the front cover. Even though the first patriotic superhero had appeared in PEP COMICS No. 1 (with the appearance of The Shield) a full year before, the impact of CAPTAIN AMERICA was tremendous, for he became "the" patriotic superhero. Like a bolt of lighting, this comic book tore across the newsstands and established beyond the shadow of a doubt the presence of a new artist (Jack Kirby) and a new character that would forever be synonymous with the Golden Age of comics. Beyond the originality of the idea for CAPTAIN AMERICA, however, it was the dynamic and figurative strength of Jack Kirby's artwork that had such a profound impact on readers. Not only were comics readers amazed, but a whole new generation of artists (both young and old) were about to apply Kirby's lessons to their own work thus changing superhero comics forever.

Comic editors and publishers had been squeamish about pitting superhero characters against the German and Japanese armed forces early in 1939 and 1940. America was still politically split down the middle over whether or not to send any direct aid to England or other parts of Europe in the fight against fascism or the threat of Japanese expansionism in China or the Pacific. President Franklin D. Roosevelt had to use the pretext of "lend lease" to supply Winston Churchill and England with goods for war production prior to December 1941. However, by the time that CAPTAIN AMERICA No. 1 was distributed in March 1941, the United States was only nine months away from Pearl Harbor and the shocking entry of America into the Second World War. By the time December 7th had rolled around, the first eight issues of CAPTAIN AMERICA had featured covers where the Nazi insignia, or some German military figure was present, and if Captain America had been caught off guard by the threat of the Japanese in the Pacific, he could always rely on FDR's classic statement: "The defeat of Germany means the defeat of Japan."

Captain America would run in a continuous series until issue No. 75 in February 1950, with three separate ATLAS issues (#'s 76-78) appearing in 1954. This popular character would re-appear in the No. 4 issue of THE AVENGERS in March of 1964, ten years after his last appearance and go on to even greater glory in the Silver Age.

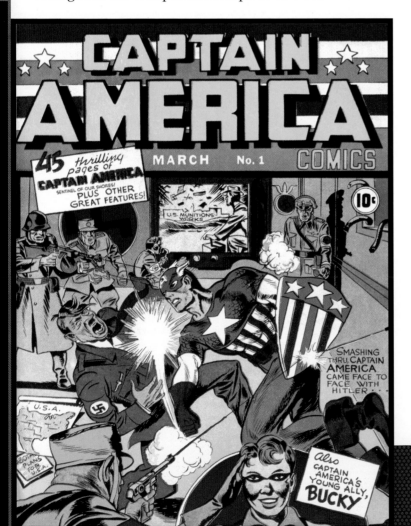

FAMOUS FUNNIES No. 1 (Series Two)

FAMOUS FUNNIES No. 1 (Series Two), dated July 1934, but distributed in May 1934, holds the important distinction of being the very first comic book to have newsstand distribution. Try to imagine the typical New York or Chicago newsstand retail person in the spring of 1934 coming upon a tied up bundle of FAMOUS FUNNIES and asking: "What's this, a funny book?" Not only was it a "funny book," but also it was for sale for 10 cents, and the newsstand retailers quickly found it sold out in most areas.

The first issue contained newspaper reprints of Mutt & Jeff (by "Bud" Fisher), Toonerville Folks (by Fontaine Fox), S'Matter Pop? (by C.M. Payne, Hairbreadth Harry (by C. W. Kahles), Nipper (by Brian White), Dixie Dungan (by John Striebel), The Bungle Family (by Harry Tuthill), Connie (by Frank Goodwin), Ben Webster , Tailspin Tommy (by Hank Forrest), The Nebbs (by W. A Carlson), Joe Palooka (by Ham Fisher) and others. FAMOUS FUNNIES editors would eventually add in the famous science fiction strip BUCK ROGERS by Dick Calkins and Philip Nowlan with issue No. 3, and thus they gained thousands of other enthusiastic readers. It's important to remember that the publisher for FAMOUS FUNNIES used as "bait" the fact that these comic section reprints encouraged readers to wait for and automatically buy the upcoming issue so that they could keep up with the story continuity! They did this much in the same way that the cliffhanger Republic movie serials encouraged audiences to return week after week, or the pulp magazine publishers took the latest installment of Edgar Rice Burroughs' THE FIGHTING MAN OF MARS and split it up into six installments. And fifty years later, younger readers would think they were seeing something new with Marvel Comics mini-series!

FAMOUS FUNNIES helped establish beyond a doubt that there was newsstand demand for a 10-cent color comic book. Printed by Eastern Color Printing Company, this comic was edited by Steven Douglass. This same man stayed the course as editor for twenty years! The first issue was a thick 64 pages, and by today's standards, the ability to produce and print this size comic with a color cover would be difficult for $5.00 a copy much less 10 cents. Douglass did use some original material with his usual mix of reprint newspaper sections, but this was kept to a minimum. Near the end of the run, the popularity of Buck Rogers got an unexpected boost when the then unknown artist Frank Frazetta produced a series of Buck Rogers masterpiece covers for issues 209 through 216! Who could have dreamed in 1953 that the original art for one of these covers (issue No. 213) would sell at auction for over $100,000! Certainly no one in the depths of the depression when comics books were for sale at 10 cents!

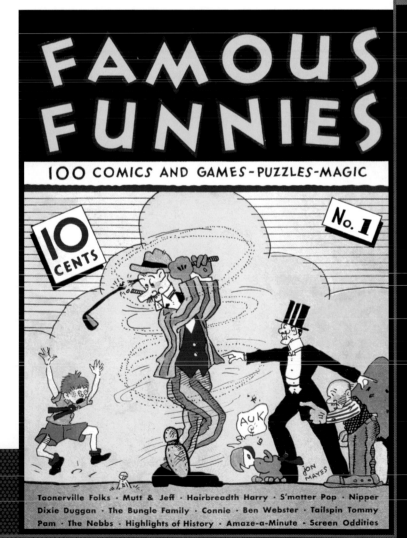

Historical Value NEAR MINT- 9.2		
1970	1985	2004
$125	$550	$27,000

THE CRYPT OF TERROR No. 17 (1950)

When television viewers watch the HBO series *Tales From The Crypt* and cringe in their chairs at the gruesome stories, or laugh aloud at the pun-filled jokes of the Crypt Keeper, a majority of them are probably not aware that this entertaining character had his beginnings within the pages of comic books. The same attributes that made the HBO series so popular also applied to the comic book stories that EC (Entertaining Comics) publisher Bill Gaines and his editor Al Feldstein brought forth when the Crypt Keeper was introduced in CRIME PATROL No. 15 in 1950: the stories were both horrible and funny! The impact of the Crypt Keeper (assisted with The Old Witch in THE HAUNT OF FEAR and the Vault Keeper in THE VAULT OF HORROR) starts in CRYPT OF TERROR No. 17 (running for three issues and continuing its numbering from CRIME PATROL) and TALES FROM THE CRYPT was profound for America in the 1950s. Inspired in part by the popular radio show "Witches' Tales," the three "GhouLunatics" brought an ironic and twisted sense of humor to the telling of each story, and it wasn't long before the three EC horror titles were selling thousands upon thousands of copies on the newsstands.

The EC emblem was a sign of quality that comic book readers could trust (for both writing and artwork), and as sales for the horror titles rose, all the other EC comic titles were carried along with them. For the first time in comics history, there was a readership buying comic book titles based on the publisher's name. This then led to the next important development, which was the beginning of the first true stages of a comic's fandom. EC printed letters with fan's addresses, thereby allowing fellow enthusiasts the ability to contact each other. EC also inspired a host of fanzines (amateur publications) and these opened the door to back issue trading (some issues were offered for the staggering sum of 50 cents!) and cross fertilization of ideas expressed in exchanged letters. The EC Fan-Addict Club was hatched at the New York offices, and club members received a brass pin, a beautiful EC patch, a card (invalid if signed!) and the colorful certificate designed by Jack Davis. In addition to all of this, members received the EC Fan Bulletin. There were club meetings in some cities, and virtually every aspect of modern fandom began here (excepting conventions). EC fandom in the 1950s, in a small and isolated way, blazed the trail for everything that was to come in the 1960s! And much of this occurred from the popularity and fame of TALES FROM THE CRYPT and the Crypt Keeper.

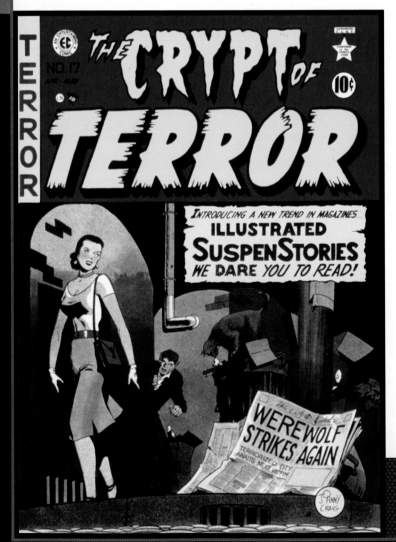

Historical Value NEAR MINT- 9.2		
1970	1985	2004
$35	$500	$10,000

DETECTIVE COMICS No. 1 will retain its historical importance for years to come because it represents so many important factors in the history of comics. This important comic book was preceded in content by pulp magazines with titles such as DETECTIVE TALES, DETECTIVE STORY MAGAZINE, BLACK MASK, and DETECTIVE FICTION WEEKLY. Its very title and the subject matter of the early issues make it the perfect cross-over title from the pre-cursors of comics, the pulp magazines. Even the cover artwork for DETECTIVE COMICS No. 1 (dated March of 1937) looks more like a detective pulp cover than that of a comic book.

Because of its early date, it is one of the rarest of all DC Comics, and finding an un-restored copy in above Fine + condition is almost impossible today. DETECTIVE COMICS also holds the distinction of being the longest running comic book title (from 1934 to present) published with continuous numbers. This comic was also the first running series to present "Original" stories and artwork in a continuous series.

Part of the reason that DETECTIVE COMICS became an immediate success is that this title appealed to children, young adults, and adults. The early covers were as serious as hardboiled detective pulps, especially Nos. 8 and 18 with their oriental themes that echoed popular pulp titles like MAGIC CARPET and ORIENTAL STORIES. The cover for No. 22 was a sign of what would quickly be approaching in the Golden Age of comics when the editors featured The Crimson Avenger (a character not unlike The Shadow) on the front cover just five issues before the advent of Batman.

It's remarkable that Vincent Sullivan, who was working previously with Whit Ellsworth for Malcolm Nicholson on NEW FUN COMICS, also did the artwork for DETECTIVE COMICS No. 1 The Asian character on the cover really isn't Fu-Manchu; it's actually Fan Gow, a character from the feature BARRY O'NEILL. Sullivan was determined in DETECTIVE to continue the process of introducing new material and he was instrumental in bringing in work by Craig Flessel and others. He had already introduced Jerry Siegel and Joe Shuster's Dr. Occult in NEW FUN COMICS No. 6 (October 1935), and eventually in MORE FUN COMICS No. 13, Dr. Occult returned by the same Cleveland youngsters.

High grade unrestored copies (VF+ or better) of this comic are extremely rare. Many of the lower and mid-grade copies were also restored in the 1970s and 1980s thus further removing collectible copies from the marketplace. Any 8.0 or above C.G.C. graded copy would now explode at public auction.

Historical Value NEAR MINT- 9.2		
1970	1985	2004
$125	$2,500	$75,000

ALL STAR COMICS No. 8

ALL-STAR COMICS No. 8 holds the historical honor of introducing the first female superhero, Wonder Woman. The nine-page feature that was added to the comic as an apparent afterthought to the usual Justice Society adventure was written by Charles Moulton, with artwork by H. G. Peter who would go on to illustrate the WONDER WOMAN comics. ALL-STAR No. 8 came out in January 1942, as did the first issue of SENSATION COMICS No. 1, which featured Wonder Woman on the cover and was issued in January 1942, with WONDER WOMAN No. 1 being issued in the summer of 1942. H. G. Peter had a distinctive style as an artist, and his unusual inking worked well with the cast of characters that appeared in the Wonder Woman stories.

Certainly, this comic character could never have been published in Japan in 1942. Women were kept in subservient positions socially or not allowed by law to become lawyers, doctors, or hold numerous other jobs. However, in the United States, "Rosie the Riveter" became the reality that none other than Yamamoto Isoroku, the Commander and Chief of the Combined Fleet for the Japanese Navy had prophesied when he told the Emperor of Japan after the attack on Pearl Harbor: "If we do not either defeat or sue the United States for peace within 6 months they will bury us, for their women (unlike ours) will go to work in the American factories and they will out-produce us in war goods within the year, and they will overwhelm us!" The man who had approved and executed the attack on Pearl Harbor couldn't have been closer to the truth, and Wonder Woman was a symbol in the American comics of why this was so.

Wonder Woman, alias Diana Prince, had her own boyfriend; she flew in the remarkable see-through Invisible Plane, and as trained by the Amazons, she was equipped with remarkable powers. Her magic lasso (a gift from her mother) was unbreakable, for it could stretch to great lengths and when encircling adversaries, it would force them to tell the truth; her bulletproof bracelets could repel bullets and other harmful assaults, and later on in her career, even her earrings aided her to be able to breathe in outer space!

Sadly, Wonder Woman's worst enemy didn't appear within the comics pages, or as a super-powered villain but in the form of a social reformer and psychologist named Frederic Wertham. When his famous book *Seduction of the Innocent* came out in the 1950s, he attacked crime and horror comics as contributing to juvenile delinquency. He did not, however, limit himself to these two genres, but also attacked the superheroes when he stated that Batman and Robin were engaged in a homosexual relationship. And what of Wonder Woman? She "had" to be a lesbian as she had a very close relationship with the Holliday Girls, and she made speeches about women becoming strong and independent, and wore sexual (bondage?) costumes of a provocative sort! Quickly thereafter, Wonder Woman was editorialized and censored into a vanilla image of her former self! A sad fate for so colorful and remarkable a character as she surely was in the Golden Age of comics.

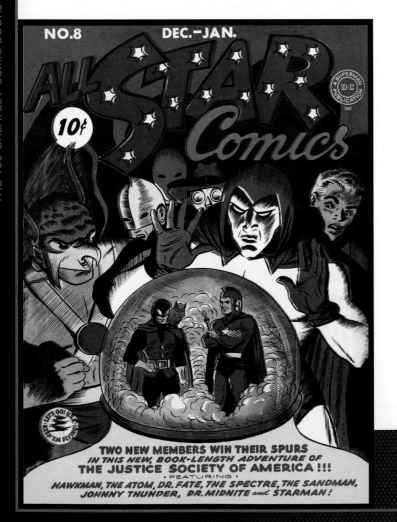

Historical Value	NEAR MINT- 9.2	
1970	1985	2004
$50	$1,000	$44,000

Julius Schwartz is one of the grand old masters in comics, and not only does he hold star status while being an editor (something almost unheard of in the artist-oriented comic world), but he is also responsible for re-igniting the Golden Age of comics and creating what we now label as the Silver Age of comics. How Schwartz did this in September/October of 1956 with the introduction of The Flash in SHOWCASE COMICS No. 4 is a story as worthy as the character itself and that important moment in time.

Schwartz began by first becoming one of the top science fiction fans while growing up in New York in the 1930s. Science fiction fandom was just beginning to form, and the very first clubs, fan gatherings, and the all-important fanzines were just beginning to develop.

A fanzine is any small press publication, self-published by amateurs, for fans. The young Schwartz was listed as Managing Editor on the very first (continuous running) science fiction fanzine *The Time Traveller* for Vol. 1 No. 1 in January of 1932, and then quickly became editor for *Fantasy Magazine* in the mid 1930s. Here he met a host of future comic book people including Otto Binder (who would write for Captain Marvel), Mort Weisinger (who would move into DC editorial offices fairly quickly), and Ray Bradbury (whose work was brilliantly adapted by EC Comics in the 1950s).

By the mid-1940s, Schwartz had left science fiction fandom and science fiction in general and moved into the offices of DC Comics as one of its writers and editors. He wrote some of the best ALL-STAR comics stories in the mid 1940s, and when the Golden Age of comics came to an end, he was still at DC as a veteran editor. During the dark years (for super-hero titles that is!) of 1950 through 1954, Schwartz was still at DC when SUPERMAN, BATMAN, ACTION, ADVENTURE, WORLD'S FINEST, and WONDER WOMAN were still being published.

So it wasn't unusual when DC began to experiment in the late 1950s with new ideas, especially with their "new-idea-introduction" title SHOWCASE, that editor Julius Schwartz would say, "Why don't we try to bring back a few of our favorite Golden Age Superheroes?" The Flash was his personal favorite, and therefore he brought in Carmine Infantino (who had illustrated some of the final issues of FLASH COMICS in the 1940s) to do the artwork, and the rest, as they say, is history! Schwartz was a purist, so when THE FLASH got his own title (after four appearances in SHOWCASE) in February/March of 1959, the seasoned Golden Age editor gave the first issue the number of 105, so that it could continue its numbering straight from the Golden Age title (that had stopped in February of 1949). Young comic readers all across America, like Gary Carter, picked up this treasured comic up in 1959 and immediately went into a fan panic! Where were the first 104 issues? But Gary, along with the rest of comics fandom, would soon find out and from Julius Schwartz and the Silver Age of comics, they would be introduced to what came before, when comics were golden!

Historical Value NEAR MINT- 9.2		
1970	1985	2004
$15	$1,200	$45,000

ARCHIE COMICS No. 1

If comics were produced for children, and if the market was designed for their satisfaction, then teenagers could not be far behind in the minds of publishers. The appearance of a new character created by Bob Montana, Archie Andrews in PEP COMICS No. 22 (December 1941) heralded the beginning of an entirely new comic book trend. Archie Andrews, the high school perennial, with his two girl friends Veronica and Betty, and his off-beat (pre-beatnik) friend Jughead would begin to fill a slot in the comic book universe that once introduced seemed to have been there forever!

By the time ARCHIE COMICS No. 1 debuted in the winter of 1942/43, there had been a year's worth of Archie stories in PEP COMICS. Bob Montana had his heart set on selling Archie to the newspaper syndicates (much like Siegel & Shuster with Superman), but he so loved the character that when MLJ Comics decided to pick up the feature, he jumped at the chance to bring his creation into print. Montana's inking style was not fully developed when the early PEP and ARCHIE issues were printed, but soon his fluid and circular organic inking came into its high style. Riverdale High School soon became the center of the universe for teenagers all over America, and the mundane antics of Archie and his pals spawned a publishing empire during the 1950s that continues to the present day.

With ARCHIE'S PAL JUGHEAD, ARCHIE'S GIRLS BETTY AND VERONICA, ARCHIE PALS 'N' GALS, ARCHIE'S MADHOUSE, and LAUGH (just a few of the titles spawned in the 1950s), it seemed as if kids could not get enough ARCHIE comics. Many a summer afternoon would be spent by many a young boy or girl, at camp, on the front porch, or under the lamp in the living room sitting on the floor, reading the monthly ARCHIE comic. What seemed to be happening with most children and teenagers is that they were given an imaginary (even though Bob Montana based his comics on his actual

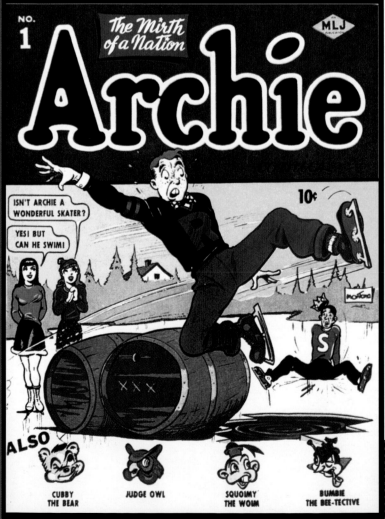

high school experiences) time and place, and a cast of characters that represented very specific personalities, and as they read ARCHIE comics, they imbued these characters with their own emotions and hopes and aspirations. Not unlike much escapist reading done in the past with Blondie, or The Gumps, or other newspaper comics, these characters seemed to be right off the block next door, neighborhood, small town, and local high school.

Two burning questions if you're a boy: did you like Veronica or Betty best? And did more girls read ARCHIE comics than boys? Two burning questions if you're a girl: did you like Archie or Reggie, or God forbid Jughead best? And were there more boys reading ARCHIE comics than there were girls?

Historical Value NEAR MINT- 9.2		
1970	1985	2004
$10	$1,000	$30,000

CLASSICS COMICS is a world unto itself within the comic book world! Not only did the appearance of CLASSICS COMICS PRESENTS THE THREE MUSKETEERS in 1941 open up a whole new set of possibilities for comic book readers, editors and artists when it appeared, but parents and teacher's associations all over America were finally given a grand example of what the comic book medium could do to educate the youth of America. CLASSICS COMICS would eventually become titled CLASSICS ILLUSTRATED with issue No. 35 (a more true description of their editorial policy), and would continue its publication well into the 1960s when the comics' market evolved past Albert Kanter's original concept for Gilberton Company publications.

The CLASSICS COMICS listings in the *Overstreet Comic Book Price Guide* take up over 13 pages! To collect and buy old copies of this title requires on the part of the buyer a patient and thorough knowledge of how one tells the important "first printings" from the later editions, sometimes numbering up to 22 different ones. Pity the collector who would strive for a complete collection (including Very Fine or Near Mint copies of each printing of each title) of Gilberton Company comics. But then, to understand how and why anyone would collect CLASSICS COMICS is to understand the neuroses and personality of the true collector! From such neuroses come some of the most important collections in the world; just ask the experts in any field. From fine art to rare coins, to vintage wine or important photographs, we owe to collectors some of our most prized and important historical holdings. You had better know your "HRN" numbers when you begin collecting the CLASSICS COMICS series (HRN numbers are the highest number on the reorder list that appeared within every single issue of this run) or you are out of luck!

CLASSICS ILLUSTRATED would introduce many of the most important and topical of the literary novels to comic readers. From Herman Melville's MOBY DICK, to Victor Hugo's LES MISERABLES, to Robert Louis Stevenson's DR. JEKYLL AND MR. HYDE, all appeared in the early numbers. Later, they would introduce such remarkable adaptations as H. G. Well's THE WAR OF THE WORLDS (Classics Illustrated No. 124), and the second edition of FRANKENSTEIN by Mary Shelly with the timeless cover painting by Norman Saunders and interior artwork by R. Webb. The introduction of painted covers by 1951 helped give CLASSIC COMICS an important new format for the marketing of its product. Many a high school student would "cheat" with their term papers by reading the CLASSICS COMICS instead of the real thing. And many new immigrants would learn their first written English from CLASSICS COMICS. Kanter's original intention of creating a tool for educating children about literature through the comics medium was not lost on the generations who grew up with the CLASSICS.

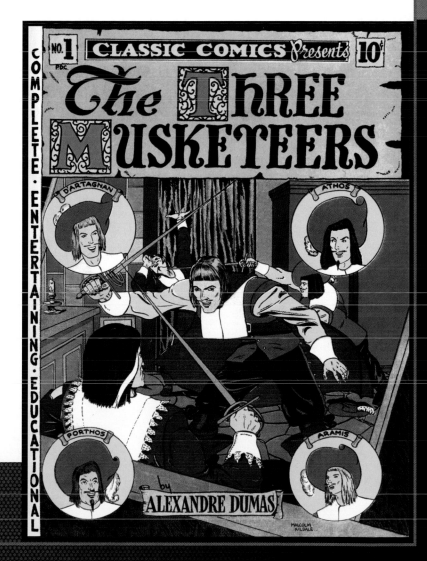

Historical Value NEAR MINT- 9.2		
1970	1985	2004
$1	$600	$8,000

DETECTIVE COMICS No. 27

With the publication of DETECTIVE COMICS No. 27 in May of 1939, DC Comics introduced its second most popular and lasting character: the Batman. Created by Bill Finger and Bob Kane, this dark and gothic figure who struck fear into the hearts of criminals was totally unique to the comics of the 1930s. Their character had its roots in the pulp magazine characters of earlier times, Finger and Kane soon polished Batman into a real comic book superhero. What made Batman so different from Superman was his atmospheric surroundings, his costume, and his necessary reliance upon his powers of deduction. Much like Arthur Conan Doyle's Sherlock Holmes, Bruce Wayne (the alter-ego of Batman) dedicated his life to studying science, while honing his body into perfection, and using his new found identity as "The Batman" to overcome his criminal opponents. This set him apart from many of the super-powered heroes of the Golden Age, and quite possibly made him more believable and interesting to his early readers.

Like Tarzan, who also came before him, Batman would swing through the urban jungle that was Gotham City; however, he would quickly gain a new set of tools such as the Batmobile, the Batplane, and other devices were introduced in subsequent issues.

Collectors have debated the rarity of DETECTIVE COMICS No. 27 vs. ACTION COMICS No. 1 since the inception of comics fandom and the very first printing of the *Overstreet Comic Price Guide* in 1970. During the 1980s the majority of dealers and collectors believed that DETECTIVE COMICS No. 27 was the rarer and truly harder to find comic book in superior condition. This is reinforced by the common sense realization that ACTION COMICS No. 1 was a No. 1 issue while Batman had his premier in DETECTIVE COMICS No. 27, which was in the middle of its early numbering. It is also known that the print runs on the No. 1 titles were usually larger. So even if the same number of people bought DETECTIVE COMICS No. 27 as did ACTION COMICS No. 1, it is very unlikely that they saved these issues the way they would have with a No. 1 copy. When we enter the arena of "condition" it's also verified that only a couple DETECTIVE COMICS No. 27s are known in true Very Fine or better (unrestored condition), while on the other hand there are probably three or four times that number of ACTION COMICS No. 1 in the same condition. Finally we come to the Allentown copy of DETECTIVE COMICS No. 27; when this comic was discovered, it sold in 1988 for the then astounding figure of $35,000 and within about three years had resold for $80,000. This copy of DETECTIVE COMICS No. 27 is as close to Near Mint/MINT as any surviving known copy of any Golden Age Key book, including the "Mile High" copy of ACTION COMICS No.1 which has writing on its cover. If this near perfect copy of DETECTIVE COMICS No. 27 were to surface in the market place today, it is possible that it is the only comic book in the world that could fetch between $700,000 and one million dollars!

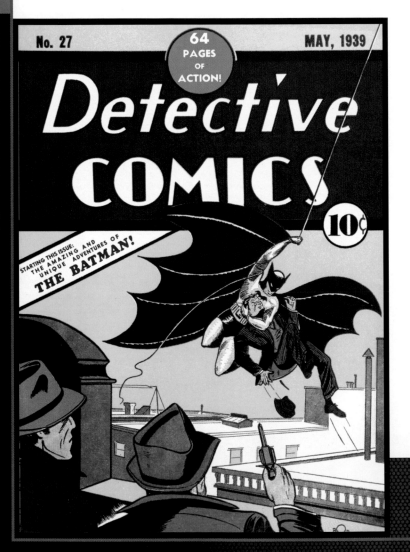

Historical Value NEAR MINT- 9.2		
1970	1985	2004
$375	$17,500	$500,000

PLANET COMICS No. 1

Science fiction has always had a presence in comic book culture. Although the first newspaper strips in America focused on domestic family situations, it wasn't long before Buck Rogers and Flash Gordon were blazing across the color panels with adventures on other worlds. Edgar Rice Burroughs' John Carter of Mars was popular in the 1930s and was reprinted in THE FUNNIES by 1939. PLANET COMICS No. 1 in January 1940 marked the beginning of a comic book dedicated to science fiction themes that would run in a continuous series. This important first issue carried a stunning cover by Golden Age artists Will Eisner and Lou Fine. The original artwork for this important title actually survived and is the only known existing cover for any of the top ranked 17 Golden Age titles (excluding MAD #1 1952); it was discovered by two comics store owners in the 1970s.

PLANET COMICS brought a kind of pulp science fiction to comic book readers. The serious early work of E.E. Smith, Ray Cummings, H.G. Wells, Murray Leinster, John W. Campbell, and other 1930s science fiction pulp authors was ignored in favor of the "western" hero, space-opera plots. The one thing in common with the pulp sci-fi magazines that PLANET did have, however, were beautiful women clad in mini-skirts or swim suits (space suits!) being attacked by aliens (or alien hordes if you will) and, of course, being defended by strong virile white men. However, it was the interior artwork that drew many of the readers and, over the course of its run, PLANET featured some of the most stunning science fiction artwork in comics. Artists as diverse as Murphy Anderson (who cut his teeth as an artist on some of his early PLANET stories and has always said that he "loved his work" for this title), Matt Baker, Lee Elias (who would go on to work with Jack Williamson on Beyond Mars), George Evans (soon to be an EC staffer), Graham Ingels (also soon to be a rising star at EC), George Tuska, John Celardo, Bob Lubbers, Bob Powell, and Lou Fine and Will Eisner, among a host of other talented individuals.

The PLANET covers are today considered classics, and also the No. 1 cover that was discovered by the two comic store owners. It eventually traded hands for a Wally Wood WEIRD SCIENCE No. 12 cover, then was traded and sold again, eventually ending up with the Alexander Gallery in New York that sold it at a San Diego Comic Book Convention for $60,000.00! Envy the current owner!

High-grade copies of PLANET COMICS No. 1 are in the market, the most famous being the Edgar Church "Mile High" copy, which was sold with the entire set of "Mile High" PLANET COMICS to a private collector.

Historical Value NEAR MINT- 9.2		
1970	1985	2004
$50	$1,250	$17,500

THE LONE RANGER (Ice Cream Mail Order Give-Away)

THE LONE RANGER no number comic was an ice cream mail order giveaway that was released in 1939 (1938 was printed on the cover, but the inside copyright date confirms 1939), and it carries the distinction of being the very first Western comic devoted to a single character. This comic book is extremely rare and seldom found in Very Fine condition or above. The *Overstreet Comic Price Guide* does not even list prices for the Very Fine or Near Mint categories because none have ever been found.

The Lone Ranger made his initial hit on radio on January 30, 1933, when it went on the air to local Michigan stations. It was such an immediate hit that within weeks the station had received over 24,000 letters from fans! Fran Striker wrote the episodes for the radio show and then wrote the scripts for the newspaper strip that followed later in 1938. However, it was *The Lone Ranger* radio show that brought fame to the character. When the radio station announced the first personal appearance of the Lone Ranger (it was expecting at most 20,000 people), the crowd of 70,000 that showed up convinced them that they could never again risk a personal appearance!

By 1938 both the newspaper comic strip illustrated by Ed Kressy and then Charles Flanders (who is more associated with the look and style of the cartoon Lone Ranger) and the Republic Pictures cliffhanger serial were released. When Republic released the serial, it ran for 15 episodes, and the Lone Ranger wore a mask that had a net pattern that extended down over his mouth. Lee Powell played the part of this first Republic serial; however, it was the TV Lone Ranger who would forever be imprinted into the hearts and minds of Americans, and this role went to Clayton Moore. Clayton Moore had starred in western films as early as 1938 when he played in *The Cowboy* from Brooklyn; however, it was his premier on

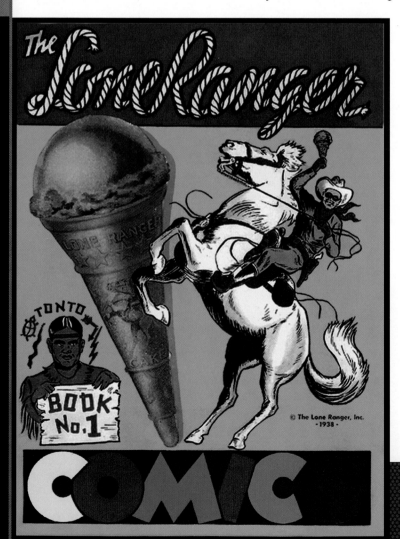

September 15, 1949, that brought the first Lone Ranger telecast to an American audience. The newspaper strip illustrated for years by Charles Flanders was one of the longest running ever, lasting in Sunday appearances until 1981.

From this first LONE RANGER ice cream giveaway comic, hundreds would eventually follow, with Dell Comics in the 1950s producing some of the most beautiful (with painted covers by Hank Hartman) examples. As the Lone Ranger himself liked to say in his special creed: "God put the firewood there but that every man must gather and light it himself."

Historical Value NEAR MINT- 9.2		
1970	1985	2004
$15	$200	$8,000

NEW YORK WORLD'S FAIR 1939

The first NEW YORK WORLD'S FAIR was distributed throughout the summer and fall of 1939 during the once-in-a-lifetime event of the New York World's Fair. This important comic book was actually published April 29th of 1939, and released on April 30th, the day the fair opened where it sold for the then unheard of sum of 25 cents. The New York World's Fair itself was a stunning success and brought to an end the era of the great depression, pre-war America, and a more quiet and simple style of life for people throughout the United States. Little did anyone know, including the young Ray Bradbury who attended the first World Science Fiction Convention in New York city that summer and had his imagination forever sparked by the wonders of this Fair, that their lives would never be the same after this event.

Not only did the New York World's Fair showcase many new found wonders of technology, but it also hosted the first comic book related to a commercial event. NEW YORK WORLD'S FAIR 1939 also set the tone for future "special" square bound annuals that would become a useful tool for the comics industry. DC had previously published THE BIG BOOK OF FUN, and THE NEW BOOK OF FUN in annual formats, but the 1939 NEW YORK WORLD'S FAIR had a paste-over 15 cent price (and sold at the fair for 25 cents). This higher price did not seem to slow down the number of copies sold. The additional fifteen cents was "big bucks" in the 1930s and the idea that people would pay extra for a larger page count and stronger cover stock (the 1939 NEW YORK WORLD'S FAIR comic had very heavy cardboard covers) was not lost on comics publishers everywhere. The comic annuals of the 1950s would all derive from this simple concept.

This early rare comic also contained the first printed appearance of The Sandman, and thus carries added weight with Golden Age collectors. Superman hosted a blond hair cut on the front cover drawn by Vincent Sullivan, with background work by Fred Guardineer who had done the cover artwork for many early issues of ACTION COMICS and ADVENTURE COMICS. The fact that this comic was advertised in other DC Comics for 25 cents presented a problem for youngsters who were about to receive copies that had the 15 cent distribution sticker on the front cover, so what did DC do? They sent out an extra comic book to these fortunate mail-order customers, which was a copy of either SUPERMAN No. 1 or No. 2! We can only wonder that anyone could have owned both comic books for 25 cents! Then again these comic wonders were just a part of the New York World's Fair in the summer and fall of 1939.

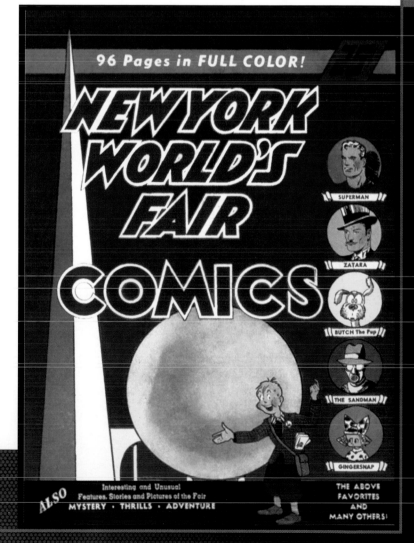

Historical Value	NEAR MINT- 9.2	
1970	1985	2004
$90	$1,000	$32,500

CAPTAIN MARVEL ADVENTURES No. 1

CAPTAIN MARVEL ADVENTURES would debut in March of 1941 and go on to become the largest selling comic book in America, eclipsed eventually by only WALT DISNEY'S COMICS & STORIES. Like Superman before him, Captain Marvel was the brainchild of a science fiction fan and writer Eando Binder. However, unlike the Superman character, which quickly became commercialized and produced by a number of different writers and artists, the stories for CAPTAIN MARVEL maintained a high degree of quality and imagination over their long run. Even though Binder did not write all the stories for CAPTAIN MARVEL ADVENTURES, he maintained editorial control over the content of other writers and saw to it that plausibility and imagination were kept in balance.

Just as C. C. Beck set the standard for the quality of Fawcett Publications artwork, Binder would help establish a level of writing that would keep CAPTAIN MARVEL readers "loyal" to their brand well into the late 1940s and early 1950s. What also set Captain Marvel apart from Superman was the fact that his super-powers were very well established early in the game, and they never changed or transformed so that a new villain or situation could be defeated. Superman at first could "leap over tall buildings" but eventually he would fly through the air. Captain Marvel, however, was put on a level "fighting" field with his super-villains and this balance again brought the level of stories up a notch and kept them from becoming predictable or shop worn. In other words, Binder and his assistant writer Will Lieberson maintained the suspense, the interest in the character, and the knowledge of the outcome of each story by keeping Captain Marvel consistent to his original super-powers.

Historical Value NEAR MINT- 9.2		
1970	1985	2004
$125	$5,000	$40,000

YOUNG ROMANCE COMICS No. 1

When Al Feldstein and Bill Gaines published the satirical "The Love Story to End All Love Stories," in MODERN LOVE No. 8 in 1950 they were actually having fun while giving credit to none other than Jack Kirby and Joe Simon, who created the first romance comic in September/October of 1947 when Prize/Headline published the first issue of YOUNG ROMANCE COMICS. It seems remarkable that comic publishers waited as long as they did to introduce a single theme title for romance comics, but when Kirby and Joe Simon developed this idea they did not have to wait for long before a willing publisher was found. Headlined "Designed for the More ADULT readers of COMICS," and given the balloon "True Love Stories" for its early issues, this comic was definitely published for an audience of women and teenage girls.

Pulp publishers had already established that fiction magazines such as BLUE BOOK, ALL-STORY, I CONFESS and LOVE ROMANCES could sell hundreds of thousands of copies to women during the depression simply printing good popular fiction with romantic themes. And it should be remembered that Edgar Rice Burrough's Tarzan was designed to fit into the women's romantic fiction market, as was "A Princess of Mars" which was published in ALL-STORY MAGAZINE as "Under the Moons of Mars" and noted as "The Romance of a Soul Gone Astray." Comics publishers knew that women were part of their core of loyal readers but it would take Simon and Kirby to address this market head on with YOUNG ROMANCE.

Jack Kirby knew all of this already, and couldn't wait to develop his story ideas within the pages of YOUNG ROMANCE. He also brought to the title some of the finest post Golden Age cover designs, inked by his veteran partner Joe Simon. This single title would eventually spawn an entire legion of romance comic titles during the 1950s and would lead to a further expansion of the comic book industry as additional readers were encouraged to buy and read and keep comic books. Alas, very few young teen-age girls saved and preserved their collections of 1950s romance comics. In today's market finding an original collection of high grade romance comics is almost impossible. Collectors and dealers will have to romance a rare blue moon, for that "dream" collection to surface!

Historical Value NEAR MINT- 9.2		
1970	1985	2004
$5	$50	$1,000

FOUR-COLOR COMICS No. 386 (First UNCLE SCROOGE)

When Dell Comics published FOUR-COLOR NO. 386 in March of 1952, it was giving Carl Barks the green light to try out a new character (previously introduced in WALT DISNEY'S COMICS & STORIES No. 98 for November of 1948) in his own title. UNCLE SCROOGE would eventually overtake WALT DISNEY'S COMICS & STORIES in sales, which is incredible considering that Uncle Scrooge was the first popular Disney character that did not originate in film cartoons!

All of this came about from the magic pen of Carl Barks. Carl had been hired by Disney in the 1930s as an animator, and he eventually was given the lead story in W.D.C. & S. for Donald Duck. It was through his creative energies (both as artist and writer) that this lead-off feature propelled W.D.C.&S. to the top selling comic book title (beyond the figures even of CAPTAIN MARVEL at its height) of all time. Known among his readers as "the good duck artist," for years he worked in total anonymity. Not only was his writing original and genuine, his organic drawing style for the ducks and their world was almost perfect for the comics medium – it would eventually propel him to the status of a folk hero among comics fans.

So by 1952 when Carl was asked to expand his repertoire to include this fairly undeveloped character, he jumped at the chance. Uncle Scrooge would eventually become a metaphor for all that Carl wanted to say about American obsessions with money, wealth, power, hard work, the desire to explore and invent, and human nature in general. Uncle Scrooge would allow Barks to continue with his book-length adventures in FOUR-COLOR using Scrooge (with "The Old Castle's Secret," and "Lost In the Andes") as a catalyst for a whole new set of directions for story plots. And Scrooge was of course the perfect opposite in chemistry of Donald Duck!

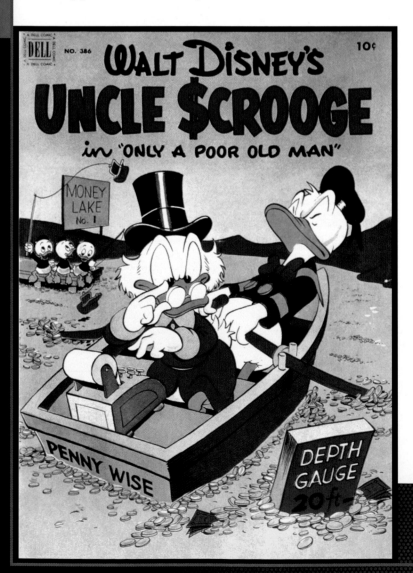

Not only did the juxtaposition of Scrooge and Donald create new plot lines, but the time honored relationship between Donald and the kids (Huey, Duey, and Louie) got a triple dose of inspiration. For not only could these three out-think and out-reason their Uncle Donald, they could also (using their Junior Woodchucks Manual) help Uncle Scrooge get out of a host of devious and dangerous situations. The kids proved that the whims and inventions of adults can use a little down to earth critical input from time to time! UNCLE SCROOGE brought to an entire generation of readers new lands with colorful geography unbounded, the opportunity to explore new cultures and languages, and the ability to witness the foibles and mistaken values of a society overly focused on material values. These were the lessons to be learned and somehow Carl Barks, Donald and his nephews, and Uncle Scrooge imparted a legion of "life's little secrets" to hundreds of thousands of readers from the 1950s up to present times.

Historical Value NEAR MINT- 9.2		
1970	1985	2004
$15	$500	$2,500

CRIME DOES NOT PAY No. 22

Why crime comics? Why did they explode in the 1940s and 1950s when they existed in only small numbers in the 1930s? How is it that American comics publishers ignored the best sources of bigger-than-life characters in the real life criminals of the 1930s, people like Baby Face Nelson, Bonnie and Clyde, Sam Dillinger, and Al Capone? The answer might lie in the fact that most comics were originally based in family situations, or on more fantastic characters (like Tarzan, Buck Rogers, Lone Ranger, and Flash Gordon), and as the comic books grew and matured, America entered World War II. The superhero surge with its obvious villains left little room for real life criminals. But you can believe that by the time the war wound down, and American G.I.s were returning home, it was obvious to publishers that more than kids were reading the funny books.

CRIME DOES NOT PAY No. 22 (June 1942) said right on its front cover: "The First Magazine of its Kind," and it was ahead of its time by several years. Not only was it ground breaking but also it didn't seem to be slanted toward children! By the second issue, the lead off story was "CRIME KINGS: The True Story of John Dillinger" (the lead narrative read: "Such men are allies of Hitler and must be treated like the low, venomous scum they are."), an 11-page feature followed two stories later by "Baby Face Nelson and the Mason City Bank Robbery." These true to life stories were the work of Charles Biro, a man who would change the comic book industry in many ways.

Biro, along with Bud Wood (who would become a crime headliner himself later in life), shepherded CRIME DOES NOT PAY through 126 issues, ending in 1955 when the Comics Code Authority effectively killed off the genre. During this 13-year run, CRIME DOES NOT PAY spawned a host of imitators, although few could top the gritty realism and hard-boiled edges that Biro and Wood provided to readers.

Biro brought to his comic work a moody, direct, and journalistic style. Editorially, Biro used real life criminal history for many of his stories. He also brought a level of violence to the comics that had never been seen before. By the advent of the 1950s with its newfound horror comics, the comics readers had already been introduced to themes of violence and horror from comic books such as CRIME DOES NOT PAY.

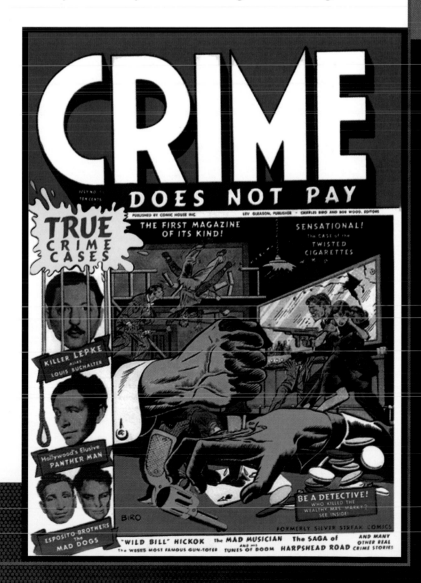

Historical Value	NEAR MINT- 9.2	
1970	1985	2004
$10	$700	$6,000

(WALT DISNEY'S MICKEY MOUSE OUTWITS THE PHANTOM BLOT)

FOUR-COLOR No. 16 (series one) presented to comics readers in 1941 the first graphic novel attempt in a Disney comic book, even though it was composed of reprints from Floyd Gottfredson's MICKEY MOUSE newspaper strip. This unusual comic book took the reader on a long journey starting with the front cover and going nonstop to the final page! Such an original idea was up to this point unseen in four-color comic books, where the majority of titles still used standard four-to-six page newspaper strip reprints or broke down the interior contents into five to six individual stories, and allowed space (traditionally the inside or back covers) for advertising.

Unlike the beginnings that Carl Barks had with his Disney character of Donald Duck, by the time that MICKEY MOUSE OUTWITS THE PHANTOM BLOT appeared in comic book form, artist Floyd Gottfredson had spent several years developing his drawing and inking style for the character of Mickey Mouse. Never before in the 1930s had the talents of a particular artist been so perfectly wed to that of the cartoon character he illustrated. The very first "Mickey Mouse" Sunday page debuted on January 10th, 1932 but it was actually drawn and written by Earl Duvall; Gottfredson, however, took over with the second Sunday installment. "Mickey Mouse" appeared in a standard 2/3rds format with "Walt Disney's Silly Symphonies" featured on the top tier of each Sunday page. Gottfredson's drawing abilities allowed him to use a traditional linear style similar to the Walt Disney animated cartoons so that Mickey Mouse did not look very different than when people viewed him on the silver screen; soon however, Gottfredson's creative talents became even more apparent. Backgrounds grew more "atmospheric" and characters seemed to have their own "rubbery" facial features and expressions, all exaggerated perfectly for the comic format but with just the right amount of linear restraint. How did he do it? Working week after week in his studio, meeting the deadlines for the daily and Sunday strip schedule (which could be punishing for any artist), Gottfredson labored with the old-fashioned work ethic. By 1938, he had brought a "sense of wonder" to each Sunday page and over time developed original story progressions for the daily newspaper appearances of Mickey Mouse.

FOUR-COLOR No. 16 was wildly popular when it appeared, and, unlike many Golden Age comics, most of the surviving copies have been lovingly read and re-read many times over, which is why the *Overstreet Price Guide* makes no price entry for either Very Fine/Near Mint or Near Mint as none are known to exist!

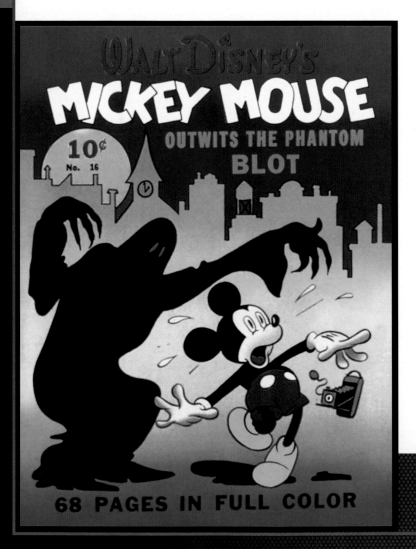

Historical Value NEAR MINT- 9.2		
1970	1985	2004
$30	$1,750	$17,000

WEIRD SCIENCE No. 12 (1950, First issue)

WEIRD SCIENCE No. 12 in May/June 1950 featured on its inside cover the announcement for EC's third horror title THE HAUNT OF FEAR No. 15 (the first issue). With this ad, comic book readers in the summer of 1950 were introduced to the twin foundations upon which EC would build its New Trend titles. The horror comics would make the money and cause the greatest social stir, while the science fiction titles would barely break even, and yet they would become timeless classics. Editor Al Feldstein illustrated the cover to WEIRD SCIENCE No. 12 and gave the lead story "Lost in the Microcosm" to the newly found talents of Harvey Kurtzman. The second story was illustrated by Harry Harrison and Wally Wood; Wood quickly developed into the "star" artist for WEIRD SCIENCE, eventually taking over cover assignments from Feldstein.

Eventually, the house ads for EC's science fiction titles would read "We at EC are Proudest of our Science fiction Magazines...Look For..." and did they have the right to be proud! Before EC and the advent of WEIRD SCIENCE and WEIRD FANTASY, comic book readers could only find pulp oriented "space opera" in the pages of four-color comics. Science fiction that attempted to maintain any serious conceptual or imaginary content was not to be found in the monthly comics. Even the Sunday newspaper strips for FLASH GORDON and BUCK ROGERS were devoid of the ideas being expounded by Isaac Asimov, Robert Heinlein, Ted Sturgeon, and a host of other authors writing for *Astounding Science Fiction* and *The Magazine of Fantasy and Science Fiction*. Publisher Bill Gaines and editor Al Feldstein changed all of that.

Gaines told Feldstein to begin reading the top science fiction magazines, and to write stories that were fantastic, full of imagination, and (more or less) scientifically plausible! Feldstein attacked his work with relish and within six issues both of the EC science fiction titles matured rapidly. In the No. 6 issue of WEIRD SCIENCE, reader Paul Gammon would write to EC's letter column "Cosmic Correspondence": "I think Wallace Wood's story, RETURN, was one of the very best science-fiction stories I have ever read...bar none...including pulps and slicks. The idea fascinated me, and I was really shocked, and a little saddened, by the unexpected twist near the end...followed by the still more unexpected punch at the finish!"

Gaines, Feldstein, Wood, and many other EC artists would continue their work with WEIRD SCIENCE. In April of 1952, Ray Bradbury found himself writing to Bill Gaines about a story EC had published entitled "Home to Stay." This story utilized uncredited plot elements from two of Bradbury's own short stories, and instead of fighting over who owed what to whom, the parties involved entered into a relationship whereby EC would adapt Bradbury's fiction for its comics. History was about to change again at EC, and its science fiction comics would take yet another step toward greatness.

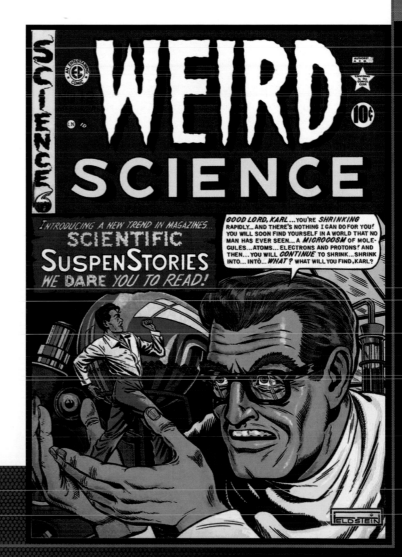

Historical Value NEAR MINT- 9.2		
1970	1985	2004
$45	$600	$8,000

ALL-AMERICAN COMICS No. 16

On the surface, the importance and originality of the character of The Green Lantern would seem somewhat questionable. ALL-AMERICAN COMICS No. 16 appeared in July of 1940 with a dramatic front cover depicting The Green Lantern about to overtake a criminal with a sub-machine gun on a steel girder, high above some metropolitan city. At first glance one might think they are looking at a derivative character based on The Batman (after all it's dark, and his cape is flying about his body), but a closer inspection of the origin story by Sheldon Moldoff (credited to Mart Dellon and Bill Finger) reveals a character of complex originality.

A literal green lantern comes by fate to Alan Scott who is about to cross a newly constructed bridge with his partner on a train. As the train proceeds, the bridge is blown up below them and all but Scott die in the accident, at which point the history of the green lantern is revealed to Scott. Long ago a meteor from deep space fell to earth in China, and the people who witnessed its arrival heard its prophecy as a green glowing metal speaks… "Three times shall I flame Green! First to bring Death! Second – to bring Life! Third – to bring Power!" After this green metal is formed into a lantern in China, and then transformed again into a modern train lantern years later in America, it falls by fate into the hands of Alan Scott. Amidst the train wreckage, this lantern now begins to glow and it speaks its prophecy to Scott and imparts to him the third Flame of Power. The lantern tells Scott that he may make a green ring from the lantern and that by touching his ring to the lantern he may renew his new-found powers. Thus is born The Green Lantern who appears in his new costume only in the final panel of this origin story!

The mythic power of this ring is very similar to J.R.R. Tolkien's "one ring to rule them all," found in the classic fantasy

tale "The Hobbit" published in England in 1937 (three years before the DC's Green Lantern). Later, it was further developed by Tolkien in his famous trilogy; the ring of power must be sought out, protected, and delivered to its origins for its destruction. However, the ring that Tolkien created was used by men for evil, and its source was evil. As the history of the Green Lantern developed in the comics, the Green Flame revealed its source as an alien race from another planet where there was an entire society devoted to peace and where there where several other Green Lanterns empowered to protect law and order and justice. Thus Tolkein's ring and Alan Scott's ring could not be more different and graphically showed how to approach an idea from both sides.

ALL-AMERICAN No. 16 carries its own power as a rare comic. Perhaps the Green Flame sought out all the high-grade copies of this early classic and faded them into mediocrity! We will never know for sure, but what we do know now is that very few Very Fine to Near Mint copies exist in un-restored condition for reasons likely similar to those suspected for DETECTIVE COMICS No. 27.

Historical Value	NEAR MINT- 9.2	
1970	1985	2004
$70	$3,500	$150,000

MOTION PICTURE FUNNNIES WEEKLY No. 1

In 1974, several copies of MOTION PICTURE FUNNIES WEEKLY No. 1, along with other related memorabilia, turned up in the estate of one Lloyd V. Jacquet. Jacquet had been involved with comics as early as 1935 when he edited the first issue of NEW FUN COMICS for National Allied Publishing Inc. (the first DC comic book). Later Jacquet assembled a staff of writers and artists to create complete books for various publishers who didn't have the resources or experience to produce comics themselves. The Jacquet shop operated at 45 West 45th Street in New York and it was here that the entire contents for both MARVEL COMICS No. 1 and MOTION PICTURE FUNNIES WEEKLY No. 1 were created. MARVEL COMICS No. 1 was created for Timely Publications, while the contents for MOTION PICTURE FUNNIES WEEKLY No. 1 were packaged and published under Jacquet's own company label, First Funnies Incorporated.

The discovery of MOTION PICTURE FUNNIES WEEKLY No. 1 in the Jacquet Estate presented a two-part surprise to organized fandom at that time, as it appeared that no one had ever seen a copy of this comic book before, thus assuring its immediate status as an extremely rare item. In addition, the comic featured the same origin and first appearance story of Bill Everett's Sub-Mariner that appeared in MARVEL COMICS No. 1, except for the last four pages, which were missing.

Close inspection of the 12-page Sub-Mariner story presented in MARVEL No. 1 revealed that the first eight pages are meant to serve as an introduction, while the additional four pages at the end appeared to be no more than an afterthought. For years the MARVEL No. 1 version had baffled historians who wondered why a blank box had been placed in the last panel at the bottom of page eight. The MOTION PICTURE No. 1 provided the answer in that this blank contained the words "continued next week."

Several other differences between the two comics eventually lead to the debate of which appeared first. Two different dated versions October and November, existed for MARVEL No. 1, while the MOTION PICTURE No. 1 was simply dated 1939, with no month indicated.

Now, nearly thirty years after the discovery of MOTION PICTURE FUNNIES WEEKLY No. 1, the debate still rages. However, it is acknowledged that MARVEL COMICS No. 1 saw newsstand distribution whereas MOTION PICTURE FUNNIES No. 1 went directly to movie theatre outlets as a test-marketing idea. Its also an interesting fact that no copy of MOTION PICTURE FUNNIES No. 1 was ever filed with the Library of Congress, or the debate might have finally been resolved!

Historical Value	NEAR MINT- 9.2	
1970	1985	2004
$5	$5,000	$27,000

FLASH COMICS No. 1 hit the newsstands in January of 1940, and brought with it the newly found talents of one of the most important early comics writers: Gardner Fox. The cover artwork was by Golden Age legend Shelly Moldolff. In the origin story, mid-western university student Jay Garrick owes his newfound powers all to taking time out for a smoke! Feeling a bit woozy from the cigarette, Jay leans backward into his laboratory equipment and knocks over an experimental glass of "hard water," is then overcome by the fumes (an early example of super-powers gained from atomics!) and viola, The Flash was born!

By the time the origin story is over in FLASH COMICS No. 1, Jay has managed to get onto and become the hero for his college football team, become acquainted with and save the life of his sweetheart Joan Williams, foil various attempts by the "Faultless Four" to steal the secret of an atomic bombardier, and establish himself as one of the most unique and original of the early superheroes in the Golden Age of comics.

The Flash shared space with equally important early Golden Age character The Hawkman, and within the first few issues their characters would alternate on cover appearances. These two superheroes would also eventually appear side-by-side fighting for justice in ALL-STAR COMICS, and would be re-developed with close ties in the Silver Age of comics. The artwork for Hawkman by Shelly Moldoff was absolutely stunning in the early issues of THE FLASH, and eventually this intriguing character would be illustrated by Joe Kubert who would years later pen the classic covers for The Hawkman in THE BRAVE & THE BOLD. Some of the Kubert covers for later issues of THE FLASH (featuring Hawkman) are among the strongest that the title enjoyed. Kubert's flamboyant inking style was a perfect continuation of the original style that Moldoff brought to the winged superhero.

The Flash would also appear in ALL-FLASH COMICS, COMIC CAVALCADE (with Wonder Woman and Green Lantern), ALL-STAR COMICS, and enjoyed a solid popularity throughout the 1940s.

The Golden Age title would end with issue No. 104, thus setting the stage for Julius Schwartz's restart with FLASH COMICS No. 105 in the Silver Age of comics.

Historical Value	NEAR MINT - 9.2	
1970	1985	2004
$150	$3,500	$125,000

WALT DISNEY'S COMICS & STORIES No. 31

The No. 31 issue of WALT DISNEY'S COMICS & STORIES (April 1943) is etched into comics history because it contains the first illustrated lead-off story by Carl Barks for Donald Duck. Carl Barks had worked previously for Disney as a gagman and animator, and he published his cartoon work in various magazines. Carl had also previously proved himself a capable comic book artist when he did work for Dell Comic's FOUR-COLOR COMICS No. 9 with Jack Hanna for "Donald Duck Finds Pirate Gold." What Barks was given in 1943 by the publishers at Dell was the lead off story for WALT DISNEY'S COMICS & STORIES which featured Donald Duck. Donald in 1943 was fairly well developed as a character; he had his own suburban home, three young nephews (Huey, Dewey, and Louie), a girlfriend named Daisy, a neighbor named Mr. Jones, and his famous wildfire temper and lack of general common sense!

What Barks brought to the table was his natural drawing abilities, his organic inking style, his ability to write about domestic situations that seemed humorous, and an innate sensibility about what was ironic and absurd in human nature. Suddenly, young children were reading stories that captured the quality of life they were experiencing each day at home, while at the same time expanding their understanding of nature, language, and personalities. It was almost too good to be true, and this unknown (all Disney artists worked in complete anonymity) artist would soon be referred to as "the good duck artist" by his thousands of readers. Not only did Barks turn Donald Duck into a real sympathetic "everyman" character but also he imbued Huey, Dewey, and Louie with an almost prescient ability to either lead Donald into trouble or get him out of it, and always with the most original story lines!

Carl is quoted as saying: "I never thought of them as ducks. I always thought of them as people." Apparently, so did his reading public, which began to grow by leaps and bounds to the point where sales on WALT DISNEY'S COMICS & STORIES overcame the monthly sales of Fawcett's popular CAPTAIN MARVEL ADVENTURES. Bark's lead feature in WALT DISNEY'S COMICS & STORIES propelled Donald Duck into the position of being the most popular comics character in America. And Barks wouldn't quit there; he soon developed Gladstone Gander, Uncle Scrooge, the infamous Beagle Boys, the Junior Woodchuck Society, Magica De Spell, and a host of other characters to widen the context of his Donald Duck stories. He said that each additional character allowed him to focus upon a different part of human nature and develop further the story ideas that he had floating around in his head. Not since the advent of George Herriman's KRAZY KAT had America witnessed such a perfect combination of writer/artist in the funny animal comic genre. And all this creative bounty came from the four-color adventures of a small family of ducks!

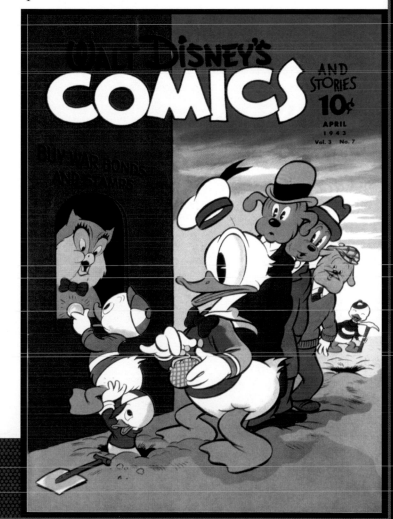

Historical Value NEAR MINT- 9.2		
1970	1985	2004
$15	$900	$4,500

FANTASTIC FOUR No. 48

Anyone who was paying attention to Marvel Comics in the early 1960s knew that something special was brewing. After years of creative stagnation, Stan Lee and his band of artists, principally Jack Kirby, began to weave a unified mythology out of their cast of characters. From the landmark FANTASTIC FOUR No. 1, it was obvious that something new had come to the comic market. But even with the creative tide that swept out from the bullpen, no one could have predicted the extreme lengths that they would go to tell a story, lengths that reached all the way to the edge of the galaxy.

Lee and Kirby had been experimenting with the previously shunned form of the continued storyline from Marvel's beginning, but they began to add real depth and multiple subplots starting in FANTASTIC FOUR No. 44 with the start of the Inhumans saga. Regardless of what fans thought of this storyline (Nos. 44-48), they were doubtless unprepared for what greeted them in the climatic issue. Instead of bringing the story arc to a dramatic conclusion, Lee and Kirby instead brought it to an abrupt halt (or rather, a dramatic pause as the subplots would meander through the book for YEARS), while jump-starting a tale that would take the comic world by storm: "The Coming of Galactus," which introduced not only the title's world-devouring namesake, but also that most complex of heroes, The Silver Surfer, who became "trapped in a world he never made."

Ironically, the Surfer was not even a part of Lee's original plot outline! When Kirby's pages were turned in, Lee was astounded to see the little, essentially pant-less, fellow zooming in and out of the panels. But Lee rose more than admirably to the occasion and began to script the dialogue for the Surfer with perhaps more feeling and less bombast that was his usual style, making the Surfer a thinking man's hero. So the Silver Surfer is "living" testimony to the success of the Marvel collaborative style of comic book creation. It took less time than the Galactus story arc to make the Surfer a fan favorite as well as the focus of Lee's fondness. The sky-rider became almost a fifth member of the FANTASTIC FOUR, making numerous appearances until FANTASTIC FOUR No. 77, when he was moved into his own title that ran for 18 issues and later, in revived form, for another 146, proving the durability of the character.

Another fact that makes FANTASTIC FOUR No. 48 so important is that it marks the beginning of Kirby's "Cosmic Era" that typified the last 25 years of his career. He turned his thoughts to ever higher planes of existence and in the 1970s turned out some of the most unique concepts in comics: NEW GODS, FOREVER PEOPLE, MISTER MIRACLE, and KAMANDI for DC, and THE ETERNALS, 2001, and MACHINE MAN for Marvel.

Historical Value NEAR MINT- 9.2		
1970	1985	2004
$1	$35	$1,500

When Bill Gaines and his new editor Al Feldstein began to toss around ideas for a new kind of comic story in 1949, little did they know their attempts to extend sales at the Educational Comics line (recently changed to Entertaining Comics) would rock the comic book world to its very foundations. What they came up with for CRIME PATROL No. 15 for December/January 1950, and then WAR AGAINST CRIME No. 10, released in the same month, was the idea of having a "horror-host" introduce a suspense story. After two consecutive test issues in each title, they knew that they were onto something big.

THE VAULT OF HORROR No. 12 (continuing its numbering from WAR AGAINST CRIME) appeared in April/May of 1950 (along with THE CRYPT OF TERROR No. 17) and was the first issue for this title.

The horror comics of the 1950s didn't pull very many punches, and after Atlas, Fawcett, Harvey, and several other comics publishers began to imitate the EC line of horror comics, things began to go down hill very quickly. For the mostly restrained and excellent artwork and writing of EC was not taken to heart by the other publishers who equated "gore" with sales at the newsstands. It wasn't long before Fredric Wertham and *Seduction of the Innocent*, and large groups of Parents and Teachers Associations began the greatest witch-hunt in comics history. Eventually, EC publisher Bill Gaines would be asked to testify at a Senate sub-committee investigation into the possible effects and harm that comics were bringing into children's lives. His most famous and unfortunate statement while under oath was when he was asked about the notorious cover for CRIME SUSPENSE STORIES No. 22. The question unfolded: " Is this good taste?" Gaines answered, "Yes – for the cover of a horror comic. I think it would be bad taste if he were holding the head a little higher so the neck would show with the blood dripping from it." The senators were not impressed.

However, for the Vault Keeper (illustrated by Johnny Craig), the Crypt Keeper (illustrated best by Jack Davis), and the Old Witch (brought to fame by Graham Ingels), their influences would live on with a series of reprint books and comics. Eventually, the appearance on TV of *Tales From The Crypt*, hosted by a rotting corpse named the Crypt Keeper, brought Bill Gaines and Al Feldstein's stories of terror to an entirely new generation of horror fans.

Knowing Gaine's remarkable ability at saving file copies (see the MAD No. 1 write up), it's interesting to note that he only saved six file copies for THE VAULT OF HORROR No. 12 (1950), and a few of these were "just" fine copies. Therefore, the "rarest" EC comic in high-grade condition is without question VAULT OF HORROR No. 12, but followed closely by TALES OF TERROR ANNUAL No. 1, for as inspired as Gaines was in saving multiple copies of his comics, he never saved the annuals, because they were reprints!

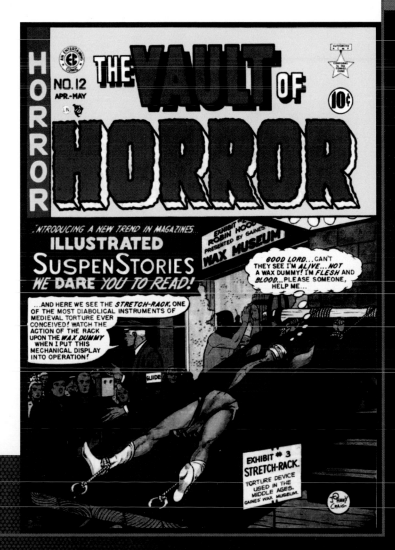

Historical Value	NEAR MINT- 9.2	
1970	1985	2004
$35	$700	$12,000

YOUNG ALLIES No. 1

YOUNG ALLIES No. 1 missed by only one year and a few months (that honor goes to DETECTIVE COMICS No. 38) the distinction of being the first comic book to introduce the Junior Side-Kick concept. However, this premier issue with artwork by Simon and Kirby does have the distinction of being the first comic book to introduce the concept of a Junior Side-Kick team. Bucky Barnes was already well established within the pages of CAPTAIN AMERICA COMICS, and Toro also had a long run with the Human Torch in MARVEL MYSTERY COMICS. The other characters of Knuckles (Percival O'Toole), Whitewash Jones, Jeff (Jefferson Sandervilt), and Tubby (Henry Tinkle) were all normal young boys without any kind of super-powers. Their first appearance (without Toro) actually took place as supporting characters in CAPTAIN AMERICA No. 4 in June of 1941, but the impact of their appearance in their own comic that same summer cannot be denied.

Called "The Sentinels of Liberty" in their very first appearance, their name was quickly changed to "The Young Allies." In their very first issue, they met dreaded and colorful Nazi villain the Red Skull, and the majority of their stories usually involved confrontations with Japanese and German forces, other villains such as "The Master of the Mummies" and the "Mummy of Death," or other equally bizarre foes.

It's no mistake that the writers were inspired by the movie success of the famous Bowery Boys (known at first as The Dead End Kids), who made their movie debut in 1937 in the film *Dead End* featuring Humphrey Bogart. After the success of this film, Warner Brothers signed the Bowery Boys (Leo Gorcey, Huntz Hall, Bobby Jordan, Gabriel Dell, Billy Halop and Bernard Punsley) to a long contract, and a series of entertaining films were soon produced co-starring such luminaries as James Cagney, Patrick O'Brien, John Garfield, and Claude Raines.

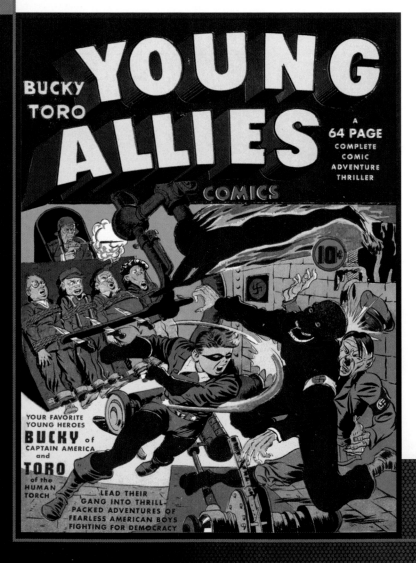

Certainly the "banter" and the lower-east side New York (at least as affected by the actors) language that was a standard part of the Bowery Boys films made its way into the scripts for the Young Allies. This attempt at bringing humor and satiric brevity into the language of the comics was important, for it would re-appear in the Silver Age in full force with such characters as the Amazing Spider-Man and the Fantastic Four who spent a great deal of time "talking trash" to the villains that they did battle with! From the original Dead End Kids, to the Young Allies, to the snappy chatter of Spider-Man, this use of language would be transformed from a colorful local slice of life, to the modern hip and pop-art voice of the Silver Age.

Although THE YOUNG ALLIES had a short run of only 20 issues, the dramatic cover artwork by Alex Schomburg on many issues and the popularity of Bucky and Toro allowed them to have a lasting effect on the history of comic books.

Historical Value NEAR MINT- 9.2		
1970	1985	2004
$50	$1,100	$22,000

GIANT SIZE X-MEN No. 1

Although they were one of Marvel's flagship titles in the early 1960s, by the spring of 1975 the X-Men were effectively in retirement. Sales on the series had been slipping, despite ground breaking work by Neal Adams, and the last issue of the book was No. 66 in 1970. Although they were seen occasionally in various Marvel titles and had their series revived in reprints, things looked grim for Marvel's mightiest mutants. And then, out of the blue, came GIANT SIZE X-MEN No. 1 with its iconic Gil Kane cover bursting off the stands right into the reader's face. The comic world would never be the same.

The key to the success of this ground breaking issue, by Len Wein and Dave Cockrum, was that it took the X-Men of old and tossed in fresh blood to bring new life to the group. In an unusual move for Marvel, four major new characters (Nightcrawler, Colossus, Storm, and Thunderbird) were introduced in the same issue. Also, and most importantly, the short hirsute Canadian "Weapon X," previously seen in INCREDIBLE HULK No. 180-182, was rechristened Wolverine and brought into the X-fold. Wein immediately left the book after the premier issue ("Who knew?" said Wein), and it fell to relative new-comer Chris Claremonet to take over the scripting reins with the next issue, the revived series with No. 94, and carry on for the next 184.5 issues; this was a 16-year run that may well be unmatched in all comic history. The early work of Cochrum was followed by that of superstar-in-the-making John Byrne with No. 108. Under the tenure of Byrne and Claremont, X-MEN would become the most popular comic book in the universe.

So why is GIANT SIZE X-MEN so important in comic history? The phenomenal success of G-S X-MEN No. 1. and the subsequent monthly series led to a mutant mania that has yet to die down. After a time, Marvel turned nearly every title into some sort of mutant showcase, and the fans still could not get enough. Even DC tried to jump on the bandwagon with titles like NEW TEEN TITANS (a team with more than passing resemblance to the X-Men) and LOBO (a rather transparent copy of Wolverine). In fact, Wolverine became one of Marvel's most popular characters, easily surpassing such stalwarts as Iron Man, Thor, and even the Fantastic Four if sales are any indication. While it is true that the story contained in GIANT SIZE X-MEN No. 1 is rather under-whelming (a giant living island), the publication of this book market was the start of Marvel's mutant agenda, which is still one of the driving forces in the comic market over 25 years later. 325 plus issues, several popular cartoon series, and two well-crafted films later, the end of the X-trail is nowhere in sight.

Historical Value NEAR MINT- 9.2		
1970	1985	2004
$0	$14	$1,300

PICTURE STORIES FROM THE BIBLE

PICTURE STORIES FROM THE BIBLE, Complete Old Testament Edition

Many people who love jazz and the early be-bop period of Charlie Parker's innovative music would be surprised to learn that among Mr. Parker's personal favorites of all his recorded albums were the "Jazz with Strings" recordings that he did in the later period of his life. Known primarily as a trail blazing and revolutionary figure within the late 1940s and early 1950s, why is it that Parker considered some of his most conservative and traditional recordings his best? By the same token, many comics collectors and historians would also be surprised to learn the following. If you asked Max Gaines, father of Bill Gaines who would later publish TALES FROM THE CRYPT and MAD, what were his personal favorites of all the comic books he launched, he would answer that they were his attempts to adapt the Bible to comic book format.

Who would believe that the same man responsible in part for the appearance of Superman in ACTION COMICS No. 1, and who would later go on to develop and publish ALL-AMERICAN COMICS, WONDER WOMAN, and other early DC favorites would have such an answer? That the same man who would then also go on to create the entire Pre-Trend EC Comics line when he was given the freedom and right to publish whatever he so wished would attempt to adapt both the Old Testament and the New Testament of the Holy Bible!

And yet, when PICTURE STORIES FROM THE BIBLE, Complete Old Testament Edition came out in December 1943, it cost a staggering 50 cents per copy. Max considered this his finest moment in the comics industry. By 1943, Max had split with DC Comics and had essentially become his own publisher. He chose at this point to produce a 232-page square back format comic book that would sell for 50 cents a copy, and flew in the face of all the commercial lessons of his peers. The results at the newsstand for this personal commitment to his own ideals were nearly a complete commercial failure. Even after the initial sales figures came in for the early editions, Max persisted in continuing this series, until it went through eight printings.

It's interesting and important to note that both Max and his son Bill (publisher of the new genre of horror comics and the iconoclastic MAD) had their own personal code of ethics as publishers. When Bill found out that the sales figures of the EC horror comics would support his commitment to the excellence of the historical war titles (edited by Harvey Kurtzman) and his science fiction titles (edited by Al Feldstein), he chose to continue publishing comic books that ran at a loss. The history of comics in America and the wider arena of popular culture were enriched by this shared heritage of ethical commitment to quality and creative originality versus profit. Inherited from father to son, from the mantle of Educational Comics to the next generation of Entertaining Comics, history would be forever transformed by Max and Bill's set of ethics.

THE 100 GREATEST COMIC BOOKS

Historical Value NEAR MINT- 9.2		
1970	1985	2004
$3	$30	$600

THE SPIRIT (WEEKLY COMIC BOOK) No. 1 (Newspaper Comic Insert)

Will Eisner has established himself as one of the seminal creative forces in comics. His influence extends far beyond his popularity as a comic book artist and writer, and the exploratory trail that he blazed with his character of the Spirit directly affected the style and approach taken by comic book artists and editors for well over three decades. Eisner started his career at the beginning of the Golden Age of comics and was responsible for forming (in partnership with Jerry Iger) the very first comic book production studio. The Eisner/Iger studio included artists Reed Crandall, Lou Fine, Bob Powell, Bob Kane, George Tuska, Benard Baily, Bob Fugitani, and Joe Kubert; all young men who would go on to establish themselves as legends in the field! This team of artists was responsible for some of the very best covers and stories created during the early 1940s. From the very beginning of Eisner's creative output, it was evident that he had a completely new approach to telling comic book stories. First and foremost, he brought to comics an analytical style that was based in the concept of telling a story by using a panel by panel breakdown that was very similar to the way a director would break down the scenes in a movie. This approach was also augmented by using lighting in specific ways within the panels, a completely new sense of humor, and a very focused sense of panel composition.

By 1940 Eisner had decided to sell his interest in the studio to Iger and move on to a completely new adventure. His idea was to produce and sell to newspapers a comic section insert that would feature his new character the Spirit. This was the perfect medium to display all of Eisner's talents to their fullest extent: ironic and mysterious, able to absorb eternal punishment from his foes, a man with absolutely no super-powers, a hero that seemed to step right out of the flickering light of a detective movie thriller. The Spirit was about to enter comics history. The character debuted in the June 2nd 1940 supplement insert for various newspapers, and continued in this format well into 1952. Eisner had created a product that brought to the newspapers a kind of comic section similar to the 10-cent comic books that children were used to buying, and the idea was an immediate success. Printed on newspaper stock, and featuring a lead story by Eisner, and two other features, this supplement also featured the artwork of Lou Fine, Bob Powell, Claus Nordling, Chuck Cuidera, and eventually Wally Wood towards the end of its run. It's a tribute to Eisner's genius that several complete collections of these weekly supplements have been saved by collectors through the years.

Historical Value NEAR MINT- 9.2		
1970	1985	2004
$10	$500	$750

FOUR-COLOR No. 74

The comic character Little Lulu was created by Marjorie Henderson Buell (Marge) who sold her first cartoon work to JUDGE MAGAZINE in the 1920s. These first cartoons were the work of a 17 year old who titled her creations "Dotty Declares." Right after her publication in JUDGE, Marge was introduced to the editor for the children's page in *The Saturday Evening Post* and spent nine years working there before debuting Little Lulu. During this period of time, Marge learned a great deal and honed her skills as a cartoonist, then when the popular character "Henry" stopped its long run in *The Post* to move into the comic strips, she was asked to create something to takes its place. It was actually a phone call from editor George Lorimer, that informed the young cartoonist that a child character would be acceptable as a replacement. Marge immediately brought in a series of (wordless) cartoons of a small girl with corkscrew curls and editor Lorimer liked them. *The Post* editorial staff came up with the name "Little Lulu," and history was in the making. Little Lulu ran for years as a popular panel cartoon in *The Saturday Evening Post* that well established her personality by the time the comic book was first brought to press.

From the "silent" and clever character of the magazine cartoons to the subtle and forceful character that comic book artist John Stanley developed for Dell Publishing company, Little Lulu, when published in FOUR-COLOR COMICS No. 74 in June of 1945, immediately began to evolve. The front cover simply showed Lulu walking her dog, and this first comic featured only the supporting characters of Alvin and Tubby (with Lulu and Alvin's mothers making their first appearance too). This comic book had O.S. on it and Dell knew what the readers did not: a one-shot comic was all that was intended unless sales demanded more appearances. The FOUR-COLOR Little Lulu No. 74 was followed by No. 97 (February 1946), No. 110 (June 1946), No. 115 (August 1946), No. 120 (October 1946), No. 131 (January 1947) , and other numbers. By 1946 it was apparent to Dell that this character was popular with readers and after a few more FOUR-COLOR Little Lulu issues, LITTLE LULU No. 1 came out in Jan./Feb. of 1948. The great and long run of John Stanley's adaptation of the Marge character was well on its way.

Readers of LITTLE LULU comics (and they sold in the thousands during the 1950s!) have the same loyalty encountered with Carl Barks' fans and they have remained loyal throughout the years. John Stanley's Lulu became a complex, inventive, always entertaining and enterprising young girl who usually got the best of "the boys" whenever they decided to cross her path. She developed her own internal mythology of characters, and in her storytelling mode as Alvin's older friend introduced some of the best children's comic stories of all time.

Historical Value NEAR MINT- 9.2		
1970	1985	2004
$7	$400	$2,250

THE AMAZING SPIDER-MAN No. 1

After the appearance of AMAZING FANTASY No. 15 in September 1962, it took Marvel Comics and Stan Lee six months to issue THE AMAZING SPIDER-MAN No. 1. This comic was released in just less than half the time that elapsed between ACTION COMICS No. 1 and SUPERMAN No. 1. But, after all, it was the 1960s and the Silver Age of comics would progress at a faster pace than the Golden Age, and no character would help propel it forward faster than Steve Ditko and Stan Lee's Spider-Man!

Of all the Marvel characters created at the beginning of the Silver Age, the Amazing Spider-Man was the most popular and original. Mr. Fantastic of the FANTASTIC FOUR looked suspiciously like Jack Cole's Golden Age Plastic Man; Johnny Storm was just the Golden Age Human Torch reborn. The invisible Girl Sue Storm, was a second rate Invisible Man; Ben Grimm, The Thing, was simply a replay from the Pre-Hero Marvel Fantasy titles. The Ant-Man a direct rip-off of the Golden Age Doll-Man, and so it went with many other Marvel characters. But with Spider-Man, Stan Lee had introduced an inspired and unique character, with an alter-ego that set the standard for this new age of comics: the Marvel Age of comics.

Peter Parker would become one of the most complex personalities ever written into the comics. Parker would doubt his own actions, he was haunted by his inability to connect with the women whom he so desperately wanted to have relationships with, he worried constantly about balancing his studies in high school and caring for his Aunt May who was dependent on him, and he never was able to assert himself in his work environment when he was up against his ridged and temperamental boss, J. Jonah Jameson, who hated Spider-Man with a passion. As original as Spider-Man was, it's interesting to note that, like Superman who worked for the *Daily Planet* and Billy Batson who worked at Radio Station WHIZ, Peter Parker would also work at a news related job.

THE AMAZING SPIDER-MAN No. 1 featured a guest appearance by the Fantastic Four, it reintroduced the origin of the character, and it introduced the Chameleon, the first of many colorful and imaginative super-villains who would do battle with Spider-Man. The classic cover artwork was one of the few times that Jack Kirby (pencils) and Steve Ditko (inks) would ever merge their artistic talents on a cover assignment.

Historical Value	NEAR MINT- 9.2	
1970	1985	2004
$20	$900	$50,000

JUMBO COMICS No. 1

JUMBO COMICS No. 1 appeared in September 1938, and a jumbo size comic it was! This large format comic book featured cover artwork by Will Eisner with interior art by Jack Kirby and Mort Meskin. The "Bigger and Better Funnies," with large pages, large pictures, and easy to read type, was designed to appeal to newsstand buyers, and it was the hope of publisher Fiction House Magazines that this size advantage would result in higher newsstand sales. However, after just eight issues, in September 1939, JUMBO COMICS became a regular size comic book. Beginning with this format change, JUMBO COMICS began to feature some of the greatest artwork for early Golden Age covers with artists such as Lou Fine, Will Eisner, Bob Powell and Zolnerowich.

JUMBO COMICS No. 15 featured a dramatic cover for the character Sheena, Queen of the Jungle by Bob Powell, and after skipping one issue (with a last superhero concept featuring The Lightning for No. 16), this female amazon would be featured on every single cover until issue No. 160, when the horror comics of the 1950s exerted their presence on the title near the end of its run. Sheena and the covers featured on JUMBO COMICS' sister title JUNGLE COMICS gave Frederick Wertham plenty to write about in the 1950s when he authored his infamous *Seduction of the Innocent*. Author Geoffrey Wagner also touched upon the notorious JUNGLE COMICS covers in his *Parade of Pleasure* published in 1955. And while both authors certainly had their right to criticize, they missed the obvious point beyond the time-honored truth that "sex sells." If it was all right to have powerful, handsome, and brave men featured in "action" on the covers of comic books and magazines, why wasn't it also all right to have powerful, beautiful (and sexy!), brave women featured on the covers of these same comics?

Known today for introducing exploitation themes in comics, JUMBO COMICS can also be remembered for showcasing some of the best and most beautifully colored covers in the Golden Age of comics.

Historical Value	NEAR MINT- 9.2	
1970	1985	2004
$80	$1,000	$24,000

FOUR-COLOR COMIC SERIES I No. 1 · DICK TRACY

The early years of the comic book medium were dominated by titles that contained primarily newspaper strip reprints. Titles such as FAMOUS FUNNIES and POPULAR COMICS sold well, as they offered readers a chance to revisit old stories or catch up on episodes missed in the daily papers. However, it took several years for the idea of a comic book containing individual newspaper strips to catch on. This delay is inexplicable as the Cupples & Leon hardcovers of the 1920s and the early 1930s had been solid sellers. Aside from the one-shot SKIPPY'S OWN BOOK OF COMICS in 1934, the earliest single character newspaper strip reprint comics appear to be two FEATURE BOOKS published by David McKay in 1937: POPEYE & THE JEEP and DICK TRACY. From these books came a flood of single character, newspaper strip reprint books, the most important of which was surely FOUR-COLOR COMICS

Dell's FOUR-COLOR COMICS (a misnomer as, although all issues were sequentially numbered, not all bore the FOUR-COLOR title) began as a color version of the FEATURE BOOKS and Dell's LARGE FEATURE COMICS. In fact, the first issue of FOUR-COLOR in 1939 was a partial reprint of the "Dick Tracy" story from FEATURE BOOKS No. 4, which was itself reprinted from the very rare (6 known copies) FEATURE BOOKS nn. The strips were from the 1935 saga of Dick Tracy vs. Boris Arson, one of the many classic tales woven for the intrepid detective by writer/artist Chester Gould. The first three issues of FOUR-COLOR were unnumbered, and Dell may have taken that many issues to decide on publishing the titles under the same series banner. Dell published FOUR-COLOR on a regular basis as a 68-page comic for 25 issues until 1942, when it began all over with "series II No. 1" for reasons unknown.

It is "series II" that is most familiar to those who grew up in the period from 1942-1962, as it continued without interruption for some 1324 issues (numbered up to 1354 but some numbers probably do not exist). This book became the feature showcase for an incredible diversity of material, ranging from strip reprints to Disney showcases to adaptations of movie and TV series. Some of the milestones featured in the FOUR-COLOR series II include "Donald Duck Finds Pirate Gold" by Carl Barks and Jack Hannah (No. 9), "Roy Rogers" (No. 38, the 1st Western comic with a photo cover), and the first comic appearance of "I Love Lucy" (No. 535). The diversity of material, coupled with the number of issues published, and the high value of the key books, suggest that very few collectors have ever tried to amass a complete set of this title. If you did achieve such a feat, however, you would be treated to a cross section of almost every genre seen in comic books all within the confines of a single title!

Historical Value	NEAR MINT- 9.2	
1970	1985	2004
$50	$500	$10,000

DONALD DUCK

The Walt Disney Company had already enjoyed financial success beyond the dreams of most comic book publishers when they began to experiment with Disney characters in comic book form during the 1930s. Their successful evolution of THE MICKEY MOUSE MAGAZINE had already established them as a force to be reckoned with on the four-color map, and they were about to continue this experimentation as the 1930s came to a close. The DONALD DUCK nn, published by Whitman during 1938 is a kind of "missing link" between where Disney had been prior to 1938, and where it was about to go as the 1940s opened up and the comic book market began to expand. Donald Duck was the second most recognizable character in the Disney roster, and his appeal to both children and adults was already well established by 1938.

The Whitman Publishing Company had already produced a great number of Walt Disney books, and held the license to all the movie cartoon characters. Whitman had printed the popular Big Little Books, the Disney Big-Big Books, and everything from Pop-Up books to early Feature Books that remained popular throughout the 1930s. Because it had long standing contracts with printers and had established its marketing patterns by the time the Feature Books came to be issued in the 1930s, it kept the same interior paper stock that was used in their Big Little Books and other publications. This paper was not much more than a cut above the paper being used in the Pulp Magazines, and while it was bleached white during the 1930s, it would yellow and turn quickly as the years went on. Therefore, all early Feature Books are extremely rare today in high grades and almost unknown with near white paper. DONALD DUCK nn today is a very scarce early Feature Book that is rare in Very Fine or better condition, and it is never found with white paper. The Donald Duck strips that were used for the inside artwork are from 1936 and 1937 and are broken down Sunday pages with art by Al Taliaferro. Taliaferro had a fine inking style, and

his brush work was delicate and refined. He certainly set the stage for how Donald Duck should look and act (in a comic book manner) before the advent of Carl Barks in WALT DISNEY'S COMICS & STORIES.

Today DONALD DUCK nn is considered the first Disney comic book. After the publication of this book, and within just a few short years, Disney would introduce WALT DISNEY'S COMICS & STORIES, which despite debuting in the superhero dominated Golden Age of comics, would also in just a few short years become the highest selling comic book in the history of comics, with Donald Duck as its star attraction over his animated friend Mickey Mouse.

Historical Value	NEAR MINT- 9.2	
1970	1985	2004
$75	$1,000	$5,000

Stan Lee had decided that the time for superheroes had come again, and when he sought the support of publisher Martin Goodman one of the first ideas he began to develop was a new superhero team. With the aid of Jack Kirby, Lee quickly came up with the formula for THE FANTASTIC FOUR. The first issue came out cover dated November 1961 and anyone picking this comic book off the newsstand (as the author did) knew that the fantasy and pre-hero comics they so dearly loved were about to come to an end.

THE FANTASTIC FOUR really did embody everything that was different and exciting about Marvel Comics. The first ten issues featured the re-appearance of the Sub-Mariner, the dramatic villain Doctor Doom (who appears to have influenced STAR WARS nemesis Darth Vader), the Hulk (when he was still dangerous), the Puppet Master, and the Impossible Man. The stories were as fantastic as the titles' name, and the artwork by famed Golden Age masters Jack Kirby (pencils) and Dick Ayers (inks) only further enhanced the wild and imaginary plots.

As beloved as the early combination of Kirby/Ayers was, it was not until later issues when Joe Sinnott began to ink Jack Kirby's pencils that some of the most remarkable, implausible, and other-worldly pages began to unfold in THE FANTASTIC FOUR. Some comics fans define their entire sense of "nostalgia" for the Silver Age from these Kirby/Sinnott issues, and they maintain that no better superhero comics were ever written or illustrated than those from this period of time.

Why THE FANTASTIC FOUR became so popular when the characters that made up their team were so unoriginal is one of the great unsolved mysteries of comics. Mr. Fantastic was a take-off of Jack Cole's Plastic Man, and his fatherly and intel-lectual qualities made him the natural leader. Sue Storm was the Invisible Girl, and though she looked a bit like a blond Jackie Kennedy, she rarely managed an original thought or action. Johnny Storm (Sue's brother) was none other than the Golden Age Torch brought back to life for the Silver Age, and Ben Grimm as the Thing was a phantom from the "monster" Big-Foot era of Marvel's previ-ous fantasy comics. But the chemistry between these characters, the absurd quality of the four of them juxtaposed against a contempo-rary environment, and the bizarre super-villains that they came up against, was all apparently just what comic book readers were look-ing for! THE FANTASTIC FOUR would become Marvel's second most important title, and is still being published today. Given the advances in movie special effects, and the current run of successful Marvel Comics movie adaptations, fans can only let their imagina-tion run wild at the prospect of a FANTASTIC FOUR movie! But as great as it might be, would it really bring back the thrill that young people experienced when they opened up and absorbed the 1960s FANTASTIC FOUR comic book pages?

Historical Value NEAR MINT- 9.2		
1970	1985	2004
$25	$1,250	$50,000

SINGLE SERIES No. 20

When SINGLE SERIES No. 20 came out in 1941, it said simply on the front cover "TARZAN – 64 PAGES IN FULL COLOR!" The front cover depicted Tarzan of the Apes, knife drawn, fighting a lion and was similar in design to the original appearance of Tarzan in THE ALL-STORY magazine for October of 1912. The artwork for that first pulp cover appearance of Tarzan was done by Clinton Pette, an accomplished painter who nonetheless would soon be forgotten by Tarzan readers in favor of the more romantic and exceptional painter, J. Allen St. John. St. John's book dust jacket art would soon become synonymous with all of Edgar Rice Burroughs' characters during the 1920s and 1930s.

Edgar Rice Burroughs had first written "Under The Moons of Mars" for THE ALL-STORY magazine in February 1912, and his character John Carter of Mars would have as much to do with the formation of all future comic superhero characters as did his second character, Tarzan of the Apes. When this author first met Jerry Siegel and talked about the writer's early years and his formation of the Superman character while he was still a teen-ager and a passionate science-fiction fan, the name of Edgar Rice Burroughs came up more than once. Not only did Tarzan affect virtually every pulp character that came after him, he was the first pulp hero character of them all! Every young writer in the Golden Age and every young artist entering into comics at the time owed a debt of gratitude to Burroughs for creating Tarzan the Ape Man.

So it was no small bill to fill when an unknown young artist by the name of Harold Foster was asked to take charge of the newspaper Sunday strip in 1931 from the first artist to illustrate "Tarzan" in the papers, Rex Maxon. Immediately the tone and content and character of the newspaper Tarzan took on a new life; here was an Ape-Man drawn in a style capable of standing side by side with the unforgettable dust jacket paintings of J. Allen St. John! Burroughs' fans rejoiced all across

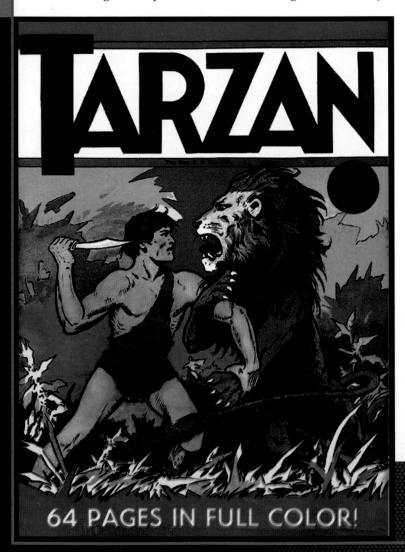

America as their favorite character was taken through a series of adventures, illustrated week to week, Sunday to Sunday in a breathtaking style that out did anything else being printed for adventure strips. Foster became so popular that young fans like Ray Bradbury began to clip and save every single Sunday section of the "Tarzan" series, and today one can still find near complete runs for sale! Harold Foster would eventually go on to create his own strip "Price Valiant" in 1937, and his fame and influence would be compounded by a factor unimaginable when he started "Tarzan."

SINGLE SERIES No. 20 had page after gorgeous page of Harold Foster artwork reprinted from the "Tarzan" Sunday pages, so by 1941, it was no surprise that all the publisher had to say was: "TARZAN – 64 PAGES IN FULL COLOR!" That's all it had to do to assure a best seller, and it's all that needs to be said now, for this classic to be included in *The 100 Greatest Comic Books*.

64 PAGES IN FULL COLOR!

Historical Value NEAR MINT- 9.2		
1970	1985	2004
$100	$450	$2,500

GENE AUTRY COMICS No. 1

Gene Autry was one of the most popular stars in America in the 1930s and 1940s. Known as "the singing cowboy," his career included radio, movies, personal appearances, and the comics, upon which his presence had a profound impact. Autry was born in Tioga, Texas, and bought his first guitar at the age of 12. He owed his first break to none other than Will Rogers, whom, after hearing Autry play, encouraged the young man to try out for radio. After breaking into radio in 1928, he almost immediately signed a record contract, but had to wait until 1931 for his first important hit song, "That Silver Haired Daddy of Mine," to make him well known to the American public. Country and Western music was still in its infancy in the 1930s and the methods of production, distribution, and radio play time for early recording artists were nothing like it is today. Autry worked hard, and by 1934 he was beginning his film career with his appearance as a singer in the Ken Maynard film *In Old Santa Fe*. Talkies had taken over from the previous "silent era" and the fact that Autry had a strong voice made him appealing to the directors in Hollywood who were looking for new talent. By 1935 he was starring in the serial *The Phantom Empire*, which was incredibly billed as a "Science Fiction Western!" Eventually he also developed a weekly CBS radio program "Melody Ranch," which ran uninterrupted from 1940 to 1956, and in one of the most dramatic moments for this show, Autry enlisted directly in the Armed Services live on-the-air!

By 1941 Autry was perhaps the most famous Western personality in America. With the appearance of GENE AUTRY COMICS No. 1 in December of 1941, the Fawcett series would last only 10 issues until 1943 to be immediately replaced by the long running Dell Series which lasted until 1959. The first Fawcett issue is extremely rare and hard to find in high grades. The early Fawcett comics also featured line drawn covers, but by the time that Dell took over the title and ran some

FOUR-COLOR tests, they were by their No. 2 issue featuring some of the most brilliant and exciting photo-Western covers ever seen on comic books. GENE AUTRY COMICS No. 1 has the distinction of being the second Western comic to feature a major character, but its long reaching effect on the comic book industry was the simple formula that established that a popular movie and radio star could dominate the sales of a comic book title if properly presented. To his legion of fans the 1950s GENE AUTRY comics will remain a favorite part of their memory of the singing cowboy.

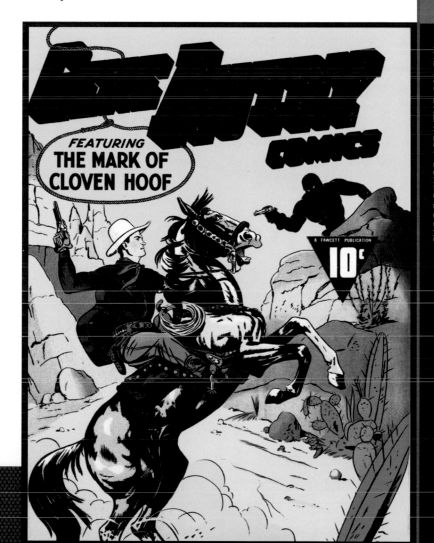

FEATURING
THE MARK OF CLOVEN HOOF

A FAWCETT PUBLICATION

10¢

Historical Value NEAR MINT- 9.2

THE BRAVE AND THE BOLD No. 28

When DC editor Julius Schwartz introduced THE BRAVE AND THE BOLD in September of 1955, this comic title was conceived as a showcase for three new characters: the Viking Prince (illustrated by Joe Kubert and Russ Heath), the Silent Knight, and the Golden Gladiator. This title would eventually also feature Robin Hood stories and it was clear that DC was attempting to appeal to readers interested in historical heroes. However, by September of 1959 the BRAVE AND THE BOLD banner was made very small and in large letters readers saw instead SUICIDE SQUAD which premiered for three continuous issues beginning with No. 25. This author remembers picking this first SUICIDE SQUAD off the newsstands, looking it over and deciding it wasn't interesting enough to purchase. And apparently other readers felt the same, as this title never took off.

However, team concepts were on the mind of Schwartz and in the same spirit that he had re-introduced the Flash in SHOWCASE COMICS in 1956, he now decided to inaugurate another Silver Age first. Having been one of DC's staff writers for important later issues of ALL-STAR COMICS, Schwartz had a soft spot in his editorial heart for this original superhero team. By issue No. 28 of THE BRAVE AND THE BOLD he was ready to re-introduce this concept to Silver Age comic book readers. He logically chose to build a team based on Silver Age DC superhero characters and picked the Green Lantern (already up and running in SHOWCASE COMICS for three issues but yet to start in his own title), Wonder Woman (who had survived the mass retirement of superheroes in the 1950s), Aquaman (who had also premiered in SHOWCASE and appeared regularly in ADVENTURE COMICS), the Flash (who had kicked off the Silver Age in SHOWCASE No. 4), and finally the Martian Manhunter (who many people attribute the real start of the Silver Age to from his first appearance

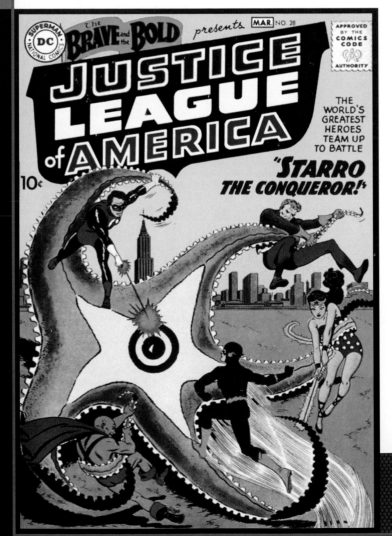

in DETECTIVE COMICS No. 225 in November of 1955). Since this was a new time and a new era, Schwartz decided to call this new team "The Justice League of America" (instead of the Golden Age Justice Society of America) and he brought in Mike Sekowski to do the artwork and Gardner F. Fox to do the scripting for these early issues.

Brought out a full year before the advent of THE FANTASTIC FOUR, The Justice League of America would be given its own title in November of 1960. Comics fans could not have been happier, especially comic historian and future Marvel editor Roy Thomas, who found the same thrill and enjoyment in reading the Justice League stories as he had earlier when he first discovered the Justice Society of America. And so fandom was again reinvigorated by one man, Julius Schwartz, a giant of a man and a "human bridge" that crossed over eras and brought to life again the great superheros of the Golden Age in new forms.

Historical Value NEAR MINT- 9.2		
1970	1985	2004
$5	$350	$8,000

THE YELLOW KID IN MCFADDEN'S FLATS

The Yellow Kid is recognized today as being the first comic strip character in America and THE YELLOW KID IN MCFADDEN'S FLATS is the first "comic book" featuring this character. Although not in the standard format of the comic book as we know it today, this book is a keystone in the "Victorian" age of comics and can be as validly called a comic book as any of today's graphic novels.

The Yellow Kid was the creation of Richard Felton (R. F.) Outcault, and first appeared in cartoons in Joseph Pulitzer's *New York World* in early 1885, although these early panel cartoons were in black and white with the Kid being only a nameless figure appearing among groups of children. Shortly thereafter, the Kid developed a life of his own, appearing in "mature" form complete with his famous nightshirt sayings in March and April of 1896 in the color panel feature "Hogan's Alley."

In the 1890s, newspapers were still the kings of media with radio far in the future and television, not even, a science fiction dream. Pulitzer's chief rival for readership was none other than William Randolph Hearst, who owned *The New York Journal*. Hearst knew very well of the popularity of "The Yellow Kid," knew that it helped sell newspapers, and so he offered Outcault enough money to leave the *World* and come over to the *Journal*. Hearst and Pulitzer were locked in such a battle for circulation that Pulitzer hired another artist to continue drawing "Hogans Alley" while Outcault moved his entire cast of characters into "McFadden's Row of Flats" and a court ruling decreed that this was perfectly legal! One of the outcomes of this very public battle between Hearst and Pulitzer was the popular idea that the phrase "yellow journalism" was derived from the tug-of-war played out with the Yellow Kid character. In fact, the phrase was used as a derogatory remark against Hearst in conjunction with a shameless self-promotional bicycle race WEEKS before The Yellow Kid moved over to his papers!

Now residing at the *Journal*, by late 1896 Outcault began to further develop the Yellow Kid character, whom he now named Mickey Dugan. Unprecedented full-color, large format pages began to appear with complicated titles like "Inauguration of the Football Season in McFadden's Row", "A Turkey Raffle in Which The Yellow Kid Exhibits Skill with the Dice" , or the magnificently printed "McFadden Flatter's Skating and Tobogganing Expedition." Running in full lithographic color, a process with rich and vivid colors that has since disappeared entirely from comics, and with the first "star" character, the comics as Americans would come to know them truly began.

Early on, the Kid appeared on buttons, inside Pulver chewing gum machines, as wooden, ceramic and cast iron figures and dolls, in special trading card sets, on postcards, and printed onto biscuit tins. In short, he was not only the first comic character but the first to be commercially developed, years ahead of Walt Disney's Mickey Mouse.

Just two years after his first appearance in the newspapers, the Kid was given his own "comic book." THE YELLOW KID IN MCFADDEN'S FLATS, was printed by the G. W. Dillingham Company in New York in 1897. It sold for 50 cents, a fortune for such a product in those days, and had a small octavo square-bound format featuring 196 pages with black and white reproductions of some of the best Sunday pages. This book also featured some original cartoons by Outcault and had longwinded narrative by E. W. Townsend. This early book is so rare, the *Overstreet Guide* only lists its top price in Fine condition. As the Kid would say, "Chee, but dat's a tuf book ta find!"

Historical Value NEAR MINT- 9.2		
1970	1985	2004
$10	$250	$11,000

THE X-MEN No. 1

As new and off-beat as Spider-Man was, it now seems that the X-Men, when they were introduced, were an even more radical idea for Marvel publisher Stan Lee. With hindsight, given the tremendous popularity of these characters when they were re-made with GIANT SIZE X-MEN No. 1 and THE UNCANNY X-MEN No. 94 (where they were involved in some of the most complicated soap-opera comic plots ever written), and the recent huge success of the movie adaptations, it's almost impossible to see how the early X-Men could have been received with such little fanfare. They were first on the stands in September of 1963, and where the Avengers looked like the rag-tag team that they were, the X-Men had the sense of something new. Jack Kirby and Sol Brodsky did the cover artwork for the first issue, with Kirby and Paul Reinman doing the artwork for the interior origin story. THE X-MEN No. 1 has one of the finest cover designs of any early Marvel Silver Age comic and the story that was presented inside made it clear that Marvel had come up with an important and unique idea for these superheroes.

The entire concept of mutants acting as a minority within society gave Stan Lee and other writers plenty of room to comment on contemporary American social norms, while at the same time using the "outsider" status of these heroes to make their plots more interesting. The early X-men were composed of Cyclops, Iceman, Beast, Angel, Marvel Girl, and Professor Xavier, but the title was actually incorrect, in that these were a group of teen-agers, who were guided by their mentor and teacher, Professor X. Somehow, Stan Lee never pushed the envelope with these teen-agers in quite the same way he managed to with Peter Parker, and this failure to further develop their depth of character might be one the reasons that the first X-Men began to slow in sales later on.   The early issues of THE X-MEN featured The Brotherhood of Evil Mutants (whose leader Magneto was reminiscent of Doctor Doom), The Sentinels (important mutant-hating robots later revisited by Neal Adams), along with a host of other villains. What's interesting to note now is how long it took Marvel to make the X-Men into a team of "really different" characters! Beginning with issue No. 49, Jim Steranko, then Barry Windsor Smith, and finally Neal Adams, infused fan interest into this title, but by issue No. 66 the last original issue appeared a victim to slow sales. Reprints were all that was offered to the fans until the X-Men were re-born with issue No. 94.

THE 100 GREATEST COMIC BOOKS

Historical Value NEAR MINT- 9.2		
1970	1985	2004
$15	$450	$16,000

Ask Silver Age legend Murphy Anderson who his favorite and most revered comic book artist of all time is and he will answer quickly "Lou Fine!" Not only does Anderson adore Fine's work in comics, but the last seven years he has done a number of classic Golden Age cover re-creations for Diamond Galleries in Baltimore, Maryland, with many of them fully inked and in full color being none other than Lou Fine covers! To talk about HIT COMICS and the Quality Comics line is to talk about Lou Fine.

Lou Fine was born in New York and attended the Grand Central Art School and later the Pratt Institute. Having suffered from polio, which crippled his leg in his childhood, he spent much of his early youth at the drawing table. He loved the work of book illustrators like N. C. Wyeth and Dean Cornwell, and a host of other early artists who had considerable impact on his early drawing style. By the time he was 24 years old he broke into the famous Will Eisner/Jerry Iger comics studio shop of artists and began illustrating comics. Some of his earliest covers were for the early numbers of JUMBO COMICS (Nos. 8-11). When Fine began his tenure with Quality Comics he did covers for HIT, THE FLAME, FANTASTIC, MYSTERY MEN, WONDERWORLD, SCIENCE COMICS, AND WEIRD COMICS. Many of these science fiction theme covers were more outstanding than anything that was appearing at the time on the more adult pulp titles such as WONDER STORIES or AMAZING STORIES, which were for adult audiences. Fine did some of his best superhero covers for HIT COMICS, including issues Nos. 1-14. Four of these early HIT COMICS covers have survived the ravages of time and are now in private collections. It should also be noted that not only did later comic artists worship Fine's work, even the young start-ups like Reed Crandall found themselves inspired to push harder to try and become more like the artist they revered – Lou Fine.

Part of the problem with Quality Comics is that it never introduced a single superhero that could stand up to Superman, Captain Marvel, or Captain America, and because of this its titles and characters have tended to fade out of sight as time passes. Only the veteran comic book collectors and the younger generation of comic book artists who continue to look back into comics history for inspiration continue to acknowledge the work of Lou Fine. But for those who do remember, and those who will in the future discover the powerful draftsmanship of this comic master, note that he should never be forgotten as long as there is a cultural and artistic interest in comics.

Historical Value NEAR MINT- 9.2		
1970	1985	2004
$50	$900	$10,000

CONAN THE BARBARIAN No. 1

When Marvel editor Roy Thomas picked up the first Lancer paperback of *Conan The Adventure* with the remarkable cover artwork by Frank Frazetta, he was doing so at the request of Martin Goodwin and Stan Lee who had both encouraged him to find out what was up with the "Sword and Sorcery" phenomenon that was sweeping across the country in the late 1960s. Goodwin told Thomas to go find a character that would develop well in the comics and offered up a staggering $150 per issue royalty for Roy to negotiate with! After reading some of the Robert E. Howard stories, Thomas felt that Conan the Barbarian was almost too rough for the comics. He therefore sought out the agent for Lin Carter and began to negotiate for the rights to the THONGER series by this well respected fantasy author.

As weeks passed and Carter's agent stalled, Roy was drawn back to Conan. After seeing the published address for Glen Lord, who was the agent for the Robert E. Howard estate, he made direct contact and, fearing that $150 per month would-n't be enough, offered the sum of $200 per issue (intending to take the extra $50 out of his own paycheck if necessary) to obtain Conan. The negotiations were successful and Thomas began to write. Knowing that *Sword and Sorcery* contained heroic action, monsters, and beautiful women, Thomas realized that he could write interesting comic stories while at the same time give an authentic flair to the Conan adaptations.

It's a forgotten fact that Marvel artist John Buscema was actually lined up to do the artwork for the first issue. Because Goodwin had agreed to the higher monthly fee of $200 that Roy had negotiated, he told the young editor that he had to find a "new" artist who could be hired for less than Marvel was paying their veteran artists. Barry Windsor Smith had done some Sword and Sorcery type sketches, and at this point in time Smith had been deported out of the United States (on 24 hours notice!) and had to move back to England. Back home in the United Kingdom, Barry was still looking for work when word came from Roy Thomas that he wanted him to do the artwork for the first issue of CONAN THE BARBARIAN.

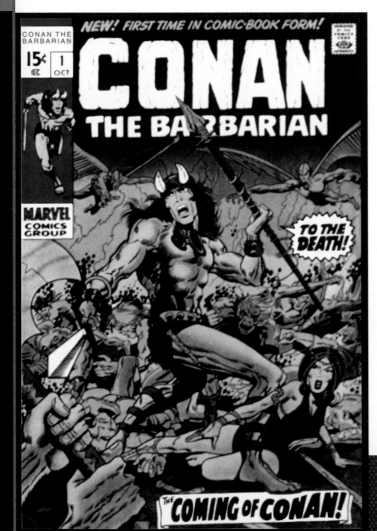

As Roy now says "it was one of those happy accidents, it was good for me, it was good for Barry, and it was good for Marvel." When the first issue of CONAN came out it was an immediate hit; however, issues 2 through 7 fell in sales issue by issue to the point where Stan Lee (who wanted to move Smith over to other superhero titles) briefly killed the title for one day! Thomas interceded, got Stan to stay the executioner's sword, and Conan continued. Eventually sales for CONAN and its companion magazine SAVAGE SWORD OF CONAN became two of Marvel's most important money makers, and the historic run of the first twenty-four issues of CONAN THE BARBARIAN, with the now famous Roy Thomas/Barry Windsor Smith team, was preserved.

Historical Value NEAR MINT- 9.2		
1970	1985	2004
$15	$75	$350

WONDER WOMAN No. 1 marks the first time in comics history where a female superhero character was given her own title. As important as it was for Superman to receive his own title (which marked a turning point in the history of comics), it's just as remarkable that within three years the Amazonian Diana Prince was also given her own comic book in the summer of 1942. The front cover showed Wonder Woman riding a white horse and leading a charge against German soldiers entrenched with a machine gun. This image made for a dramatic patriotic cover, but in reality it looked more like a scene out of World War I than World War II, which was being fought with far different tactics.

The first issue of WONDER WOMAN presented a much more developed origin story than was given in ALL-STAR No. 8 (Wonder Woman's first appearance , which then became the second highest selling comic of all time), and had four complete stories illustrated by artist H. G. Peter. Viewed from the distance of time it's apparent that Wonder Woman, unlike Superman, was created by a small committee of editors, and many of the characteristics we associate with her were projections of how "men" thought a female superhero should act. Wonder Woman's actual creator, William Moulton Marston, was already an accomplished individual having developed the systolic blood-pressure test which lead to the creation of the polygraph, better know today as the lie detector. Marston also happened to champion the causes of women and when he met Max Gaines, asked why there was not a strong female superhero in comics. Gaines was interested enough to give Marston a challenge: create a woman wonder, a superhero for women! Marston did so using Max's middle-name, and created his pen name of Charles Moulton for the comic book publication.

The combination of Marston's historical mythology that surrounded Princess Diana, and the eccentric originality of H. G. Peter's artwork were enough to draw in a large number of readers and keep them coming back to buy SENSATION COMICS, ALL-STAR COMICS, COMICS CAVALCADE, and eventually WONDER WOMAN. Despite her critics and other detractors, she also leapt over the Comics Code Authority and the Dark Ages of the mid 1950s when, along with Superman, the Batman & Robin, Blackhawk, and Superboy, she was the only other superhero character to remain in print when the entire Golden Age of superheros were temporally relegated into the dust bin of history! So, there must have been a large and faithful readership, and it couldn't have been composed only of young boys and men who had hidden fantasies about powerful women in costumes!

Historical Value	NEAR MINT- 9.2	
1970	1985	2004
$50	$1,000	$34,000

3-D COMICS, TOR No. 1

The 1920s brought forth bobbed hair, liquor in flasks at football games, and the 1929 Stock Market Crash; the 1930s gave America radio at its height, prohibition, and the Great Depression; the 1940s acknowledged fascism in Europe, the big bands and swing, and the atomic bomb; by the 1950s, Americans were ready for the suburbs, television, rock and roll, and prosperity. So it's no wonder that a number of popular cultural breakthroughs took place in the "staid" 1950s. The 3-D craze was part of this period of time, and it began in the movie industry when studio executives began to worry that television would drain the number of movie attending audiences. 3-D movies had been experimented with before by Hollywood but with no great success. Now with improved projectors and more refined movie theaters the industry was willing to try again and on November 26, 1952 the premier for *Bwana Devil* hit the theaters. The idea that audiences would go into a dark theater and put on colored glasses was enough of a gimmick that eventually other movies followed, with two of the best being *Kiss Me Kate* and *It Came From Outer Space*. Though these films gave some movie viewers headaches, and were complicated by the requirement that two projectors were required, to be run in perfect harmony, the 3-D craze was off and running.

Comics publishers looked at all of this and realized that the printing process for 3-D was no more expensive and it in fact, threw out the window the requirement of four-color printing and replaced it with three colors: green, red, and black or brown. But what they didn't take into account was the complicated process that the artists had to go through to finish the pre-production original artwork! The artists would begin by pencilling their layout and placement; they then had to work on celluloid sheets or cels (much like movie animation artists used) and identify and separately draw each figure, object, and background (each on a different layer of celluloid) that they wanted to appear for each different level. This process required back-breaking concentration and hours of work all just for a single story! When the first 3-D comic books came out, they were met with enthusiasm, but the problem seemed to be that once experienced by children they became passe. 3-D COMICS, TOR No. 1 was a beautiful example published by St. John Publishers and illustrated by Golden Age great Joe Kubert. The comics experienced the same problems as the films however, in that if the printed registration for the green and red lines (with the brown) was off by too much then the 3-D image blurred, and after one or two efforts by most companies (EC Comics did two 3-D comics, DC also just two), the fad had spent itself.

Today, 3-D comics are highly prized collectors items, and what single common denominator makes them so expensive? Well, of course, they have to be found with the 3-D glasses intact! What self respecting child would buy one of these comics in the 1950s and not remove the glasses so that they could read the comic book? Not many!

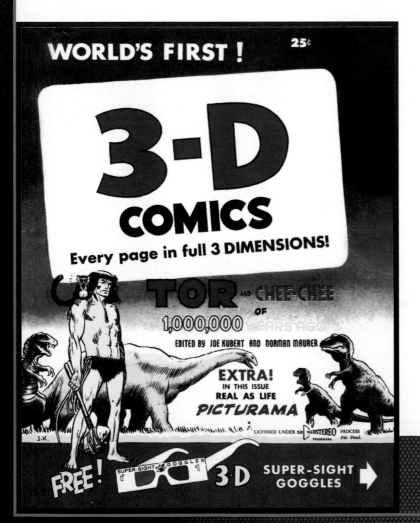

Historical Value NEAR MINT- 9.2		
1970	1985	2004
$12	$75	$250

THUNDA KING OF THE CONGO No. 1

The history of comics is rich with examples of artists striving for and attaining greatness. As diverse and remarkable as many of these artists are, none of them went through the transformations, changes and eventual fame of Frank Frazetta. Frazetta is the only comic artist with major listings in all three chapters of *The Comic Art Price Guide*: first is his newspaper strip *Johnny Comet* (Frazetta also ghosted for "LI'L ABNER"), second for his 1950s comic book work, and third with the science fiction chapter for his inspired paperback and magazine paintings. Frank Frazetta was born in Brooklyn in 1928 and grew up knowing that he would some day become an artist. He enrolled in the Brooklyn Academy of Fine Arts when he was only eight. His first published comic art was in TALLY HO (for Snowman) when he was only sixteen. Eventually doing several early cartoons in funny animal comics, his style began to mature and by the early 1950s his comic book stories for DAN BRAND AND TIPI, THUNDA, the FAMOUS FUNNIES covers, and his work with the "Fleagles" (Angelo Torres, Al Williamson, Nick Meglin and Roy G. Krenkel) gang at EC Comics had already made him famous in the comic book world.

Most artists would quit right there, but Frazetta always dreamed of having his own strip and so he developed JOHNNY COMET, and after EC also did ghosting for Al Capp's "Li'l Abner" newspaper strip. It was during this period of time in the late 1950s and early 1960s that Frazetta continued his friendships with other artists, including Roy G. Krenkel. Krenkel was an avid Edgar Rice Burroughs and Robert E. Howard fan who was constantly doing free illustrations for George Scither's AMRA (a Sword & Sorcery fanzine), and knew many people in the science fiction world. Because of his connections, he was asked by Donald Wollheim (the editor at Ace Books) to begin work on a new series of paperback covers for Burroughs' books. Roy went to Frazetta for help and inspiration and the rest as they say, is history. Frazetta became, within a short period of

four years, the leading fantasy and science fiction and horror paperback cover artist in America, helped along by his masterfully painted covers for the Warren Magazines CREEPY and EERIE. However, it was Robert E. Howard's CONAN that changed Frazetta's artistic life forever. When Lancer books contacted Frank to do the covers for a new series of Conan paperback covers, Frank decided that he had just been playing around with the Ace Burroughs' covers, and he wanted to put his own personal stamp on a part of illustration history. Frazetta decided that he would give the Conan paperback covers all that he had. All of a sudden he was right up there at the top, alongside the artists of his childhood, N. C. Wyeth and Frank Scoonover, and all this from a beginning in four-color comics! THUNDA No. 1 was produced by Frazetta in the middle of his comic career in 1952 for Magazine Enterprises, and was the perfect blend of his powerful inking style and his lifetime interest in the works of Edgar Rice Burroughs' character Tarzan of the Apes.

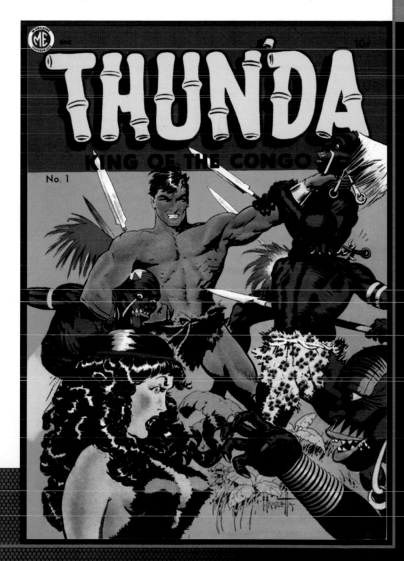

Historical Value NEAR MINT- 9.2		
1970	1985	2004
$30	$800	$2,500

CRIME SUSPENSTORIES No. 22

Never has a single comic book carried the status of having the most "infamous" comic cover of all time, while also representing the rights of freedom of expression and freedom from censorship that CRIME SUSPENSTORIES No. 22 brings to any debate about comics. EC Comics, the small and enterprising group of editors, writers and artists who were banded together by publisher Bill Gaines in the 1950s managed to change the entire course of comics history in just four short years. They created the most serious and mature science fiction comics ever witnessed. They brought forth the almost unimaginable concept of war comics that could possibly cause readers to become pacifists after only one reading. And they addressed the social taboos such as police brutality (adult policemen taking sexual advantage of teen-age girls!), racial hatred, corruption in the press, and hard core drug abuse in their suspense titles. Beyond social taboos, EC also created and developed the modern horror comics, and were probably primarily responsible for bringing down the senate investigations and the eventual formation of the Comic Code Authority that lead to their death. And on top of this they gave the world MAD. The greatest satire comic (and magazine) ever published! The comic book MAD escaped the Comics Code Authority when it was remade into a magazine with issue No. 24 and went on to even greater fame and sales figures while forever transforming American youth.

CRIME SUSPENSTORIES and SHOCK SUSPENSTORIES were the titles that EC created at the height of its popularity to contain a "mix" of content. The early covers for CRIME SUSPENSTORIES were quite restrained though the first 14 issues. However with Nos. 15 and 16 they began to look like covers to the horror titles, and with issue No. 17 a man was shown blowing his brains out right in front of his wife. CRIME SUSPENSTORIES No. 19 depicted a woman being strangled under water, and No. 20 featured a hanged man, but it was issue No. 22 that really pressed the envelope when it showed a man holding the

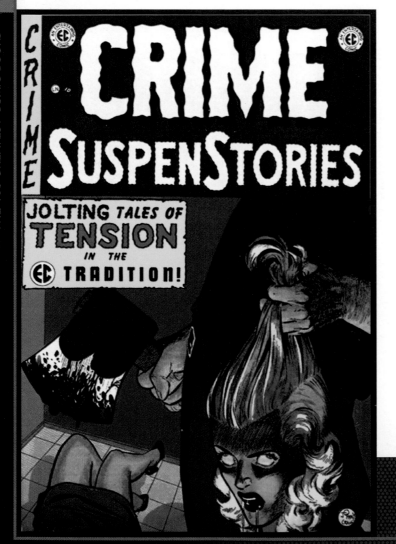

severed head of a woman in his left hand while his right hand held the bloody ax. Even Stephen King would have had nightmares as a child!

Publisher Gaines would eventually be confronted by the New York Senate Subcommittee investigating juvenile delinquency on April 21, 1954. Gaines appeared as a voluntary witness and after introducing himself and giving the subcommittee a short history of his father Max's involvement in comics opened himself up to questioning. These hearings were on television, and after some time the questions came around to the cover for CRIME SUSPENSTORIES No. 22. Gaines was asked if this cover was within the bounds of good taste. He answered that yes, it was, for the cover of a horror comic, and that if the head was slightly higher so that the neck could be seen dripping blood and if the body was viewed a little further so that the neck could be seen it would have been bad taste. Based on today's standards with modern slasher and action films and the high level of violence on TV, this cover now seems almost sedate, but in 1954 it was enough for the Senators and the television viewing audience to decide against horror and crime comics. The era of EC's dominance in the comic industry was about to draw to a close.

Historical Value	NEAR MINT- 9.2	
1970	1985	2004
$5	$75	$700

STRANGE ADVENTURES No. 1

When STRANGE ADVENTURES No. 1 appeared in August/September 1950, it was the culmination of years of experience and friendships for editor Julius Schwartz. Schwartz grew up in Brooklyn during the 1930s as a staunch science fiction fan and was among the leading personalities of his time, contributing to a number of early important fan publications and eventually acting as agent for many early science fiction writers including Stanley G. Weinbaum and Ray Bradbury. As editor, Schwartz looked to showcase already established science fiction authors within the pages of STRANGE ADVENTURES, using the talents of Otto Binder, Leigh Brackett, John Broome, Gardner F. Fox, Horace Gold (who would later become editor for GALAXY SCIENCE FICTION), Sam Merwin, and Edmond Hamilton. Not only did Schwartz acquire some of the finest science fiction authors to write his stories, but also he brought in such artists as Murphy Anderson, Gil Kane, Frank Frazetta (for the companion title MYSTERY IN SPACE), Carmine Infantino, Bernard Krigstein, Lee Elias, John Guinta, and even the renowned Virgil Finlay, to illustrate these stories.

STRANGE ADVENTURES escaped the death throes caused by the Comics Code Authority, and when other publishers were going out of business (including EC Comics), this title survived and continued well into the 1970s. STRANGE ADVENTURES No. 1 featured the only photo cover for this title, and its dramatic picture of a scene from the movie for Robert Heinlein's DESTINATION MOON has turned the first issue into a collector's item. Thereafter, STRANGE ADVENTURES would feature the longest running string of excellent science fiction covers ever to grace a comic book, including the PLANET COMICS run. Murphy Anderson, Carmine Infantino, and Gil Kane would account for the majority of these masterful and unique science fiction covers, and today the entire run is appreciated for its overall excellence and the original thrills that were brought to young readers all the way from 1950 to 1973.

STRANGE ADVENTURES also published a lively letters page, and just as EC had done over on Lafayette Avenue with its fan letters, Schwartz printed the names and addresses of his correspondents knowing full well that this simple act was the foundation for the original science fiction fandom of the 1930s. Schwartz would within six years re-introduce readers to the Flash and thus ignite the Silver Age of comics. But before this ground breaking event, he laid his own foundation for excellence with his 1950s science fiction comics proving once again that as visual as the comics medium was (and dependent upon the skills of its artists for sales), first and foremost they had to have well-written stories. Julius Schwartz and STRANGE ADVENTURES more than filled the bill in the 1950s, and his place in comics history is only further enhanced by the science fiction stories that gave his comics their own special "sense of wonder."

Historical Value NEAR MINT - 9.2		
1970	1985	2004
$10	$400	$5,000

GREEN LANTERN NO. 76

When DC Comics convinced its new artist Neal Adams to begin illustrating THE GREEN LANTERN beginning with issue No. 76, it could not have been fully prepared for the response in the market place. Neal Adams had previously done a short series for DC in STRANGE ADVENTURES with the character Deadman in Nos. 206-216, and his powerful presence had been noted by comic readers. He had developed his drawing style while working anonymously during the 1960s doing daily strips for RIP KIRBY and PETER SCRATCH, so by the time he came to DC in 1967, he had a fully honed and mature style. Adams is important to comics for a number of reasons, the first being that he was part of a new generation of artists who began to change the course, and directly affect the volume of sales, of specific characters and titles that they chose to work on. By the time Adams had finished his dramatic series of stories for THE GREEN LANTERN, he had changed the minor character of the Green Arrow into a major character, and brought comics fans to their knees by the end of his stint with issue No. 89. Neal Adams had over-night become the Frank Frazetta of comics, for any comic book title he chose to work on experienced an instant jump in sales figures!

Adams would go on to infuse life into Marvel's THE X-MEN and THE AVENGERS, render dramatic and original covers for DETECTIVE COMICS and BATMAN, and breathe life into a number of different comic titles. He would eventually go on to found Continuity Comics in 1987. However, his second most important contribution to mainstream comics was his persistent and stubborn pursuit of the major publishers to open up better creator rights agreements for both writers and artists. The Underground Comix revolution had already started to take place in 1967 when Adams first began to work for DC Comics, and it was well known throughout the professional mainstream field that the Underground Comix artists (at

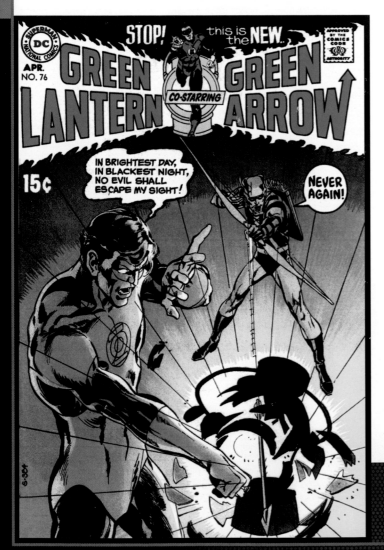

least a good majority of them!) were enjoying copyright ownership of their characters, reprint and royalty payments on all comics reprinted, and the option to develop their characters with movies or toys on their own. Not only did these artists have all the aforementioned rights, but they received back from the publisher 100% of all their original artwork! Adams took this Underground Comix idea of creator rights into the offices of DC and Marvel, and eventually he won! Hundreds of pages of original artwork were returned to Jack Kirby, Dick Ayers, John Romita, and host of other artists. Not only did Adams get concessions for artists, he managed to negotiate a symbolic financial recognition for Jerry Siegel and Joe Shuster from DC for their original creation of the character Superman. Neal Adams had not only won the hearts and minds of the comics fans, but he went on to gain the respect and admiration of everyone who was ever connected with comics with his activism for creator rights.

Historical Value NEAR MINT- 9.2		
1970	1985	2004
$1	$75	$350

Other than Tarzan of the Apes, the one pulp character that exerted the most influence on the formation and creation of many Golden Age comics' characters was the Shadow. The tale of his own birth is a strange story and begins well before Walter Gibson wrote the first Shadow stories for the first issue of the pulp magazine to the time when the Shadow was created by committee. In 1929 Street & Smith ran a very popular series of stories in their DETECTIVE STORY MAGAZINE that eventually was adapted to be read on radio. Radio was at the height of its economic reach and also experienced its greatest popularity in depression-era America. As the detective stories unfolded on this radio show, the person who was reading them began to be called "The Shadow," and it wasn't long before other radio stations copied the format with "The Mysterious Traveler " and "The Whistler." Now Street & Smith had a problem as they needed to copyright and protect their new-found character, but they didn't know if they could copyright an on-air personality! Their solution was to begin a special contest in the pages of DETECTIVE STORY MAGAZINE, giving clues as to what the Shadow looked like and what kind of character he was. The readers were encouraged to send in their own conclusions, and Street & Smith then published the names of the winners and announced that they would print a one-shot magazine using the results.

Walter Gibson was given the winning ideas, and immediately rejected most of what was submitted by the fans! He went on to finish the stories for the first April 1931 issue of THE SHADOW: A DETECTIVE MAGAZINE. This first issue sold out in several days, was then scheduled by Street & Smith as a quarterly magazine (after they had secured their copyright!), and quickly became a bi-monthly. It was a smash HIT in the pulp magazine world! Known throughout the world for his famous lines "who knows what evil lurks in the hearts of men…" and "the weed of crime bears bitter fruit," this

character was eventually published by Street and Smith as a four-color comic book in March of 1940. The first six issues of SHADOW COMICS featured pulp-style cover paintings before a switch over to line-drawn covers for the remainder of the run was made.

SHADOW COMICS featured some fine covers by comic artist Bob Powell, included a series of exciting stories illustrated by Vernon Greene, and continued to exert an influence on the comics publishing industry throughout the 1940s. The Batman himself, the Spectre, and a host of other Golden Age comic superheroes owed the genesis of their creation to the ideas in Walter Gibson's Shadow stories, and the comics were further enriched by this dark hero who fought crime with the powers of his mind and his own cunning.

Historical Value NEAR MINT- 9.2		
1970	1985	2004
$50	$500	$8,000

HOT ROD COMICS (First issue)

In the dawning 1950s, American youth was rebellious, yet affluent enough not only to afford their own automobiles, but to modify them to a point where the cars actually defined their generation. Vehicles were restored (many were from the 1930s), reshaped (chopped and channeled were terms describing the work), and rebuilt (specifically the engines, which were created for maximum speed). Hot-Rod culture had a powerful impact on the country and manifested itself in a myriad of ways, from expressive street jargon ("Cool set of wheels, man! My short's in the garage!") to media phenomena (hot-rod magazines flooded the newsstands) - - including a wave of movies and comic books.

The publication that scored top trophy in the dragstrip wars was Fawcett's HOT ROD COMICS (a somewhat surprising entry for a company that sported a conservative editorial policy and predicated much of their comics lineup on AAA-rated Hollywood personalities). Brandishing the definitive genre title, the cover for the first issue accelerated readers right into the action with a pair of street rods barreling along a concrete speedway under a checkered flag and a target blurb that proclaimed: "Souped Up Action on a Hot Set of Wheels!"

Fans have never quite figured out why the first issue was unnumbered and undated, but a little logic suggests that the publishers were not convinced a market could be found, so the comic was printed as a one-shot. The premise and the characters established in the first issue, however, indicate that sufficient thought had been invested in the possibility of a series, one not unlike "Andy Hardy Lays Rubber."

The titles most remarkable achievement, however, was its integration of plot action and technical detail (which always puts the brakes on any narrative motion). In the lead tale, for example, Curtis buys and converts a junkyard wreck into a cool street machine and the step-by-step process is revealed in a double-page, collage-like sequence without panels. What made it - - and the entire series - - so believable was the photographic depiction of engines, suspension systems, parts, and tools, an extremely demanding task that could only have been accomplished by top pros, in this case, Bob Powell assisted by Howard Nostrand on backgrounds.

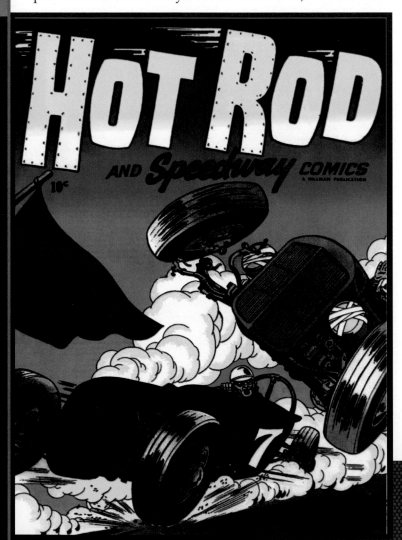

Both HOT ROD COMICS and HOT RODS AND RACING CARS peeled out simultaneously, using 11/51 as their starting line, and were followed by such titles as SPEED SMITH, HOT ROD AND SPEEDWAY COMICS, and HOT ROD KING, and two decades later, HOT WHEELS. They all slammed into high gear to exploit the craze of greasemonkey kids with double-clutch fever, most of which predictably ran out of gas after a couple years of over-revved action. HOT ROD RACERS managed to stay on the track from 1964-67, then required a paint job to emerge as GRAND PRIX, which finally stalled in 1970. HR&RC got the checkered flag as the title with the most laps and eventually made its final pit stop in 1973.

Historical Value NEAR MINT- 9.2		
1970	1985	2004
$1	$25	$450

Carmine Infantino best represented the contrast between Silver Age DC Comics and those being produced by Stan Lee for Marvel Comics. Infantino's artwork for the sophisticated character of the Flash stood in marked contrast to the brazen and hyped-up covers that readers viewed on the early FANTASTIC FOUR numbers. Was comics fandom split between "adult" readers and thrill-seekers? Probably not, but you couldn't convince some of the most ardent fans who loved the work of Carmine Infantino and Murphy Anderson above all others during the early 1960s.

When Julius Schwartz made the fateful decision to feature the re-imagined Golden Age Flash in SHOWCASE No. 4 in 1956, he quickly followed up with three additional SHOWCASE appearances, at which point it was decided to give the Flash his own title. In February/March of 1959 THE FLASH No. 105 hit the newsstands, continuing its original numbering from the very last issue of the Golden Age FLASH COMICS. The new Flash had a more streamlined costume (he didn't wear the cumbersome hat that the Golden Age Flash did), and the refined line work that Infantino was capable of only seemed to embellish what the editors were trying to accomplish with each succeeding cover concept. Whereas the Golden Age Flash covers seemed to be scenes frozen in time, the Infantino covers almost caused the wind to brush against the readers face as they viewed the Flash in action. Not only was the Silver Age Flash drawn better, but the new alter-ego for the Flash, Barry Allen, had a more interesting background and brought more to the table as each story unfolded. The DC readers now felt that they had a character that was both exciting and believable, a combination that they were convinced Marvel did not have a handle on!

And in addition to all this, the villains continued the new found tradition of respectability as the Mirror Master, the Pied Piper, the Trickster, Captain Boomerang and more, all paraded forth with conservative and urbane personalities. Perhaps editor Julius Schwartz was aware of all of this when he presented "The Flash of Two Worlds" wherein he brought back the Golden Age Flash to help his Silver Age counterpart in a special one issue story for THE FLASH No. 123. This famous story also introduced for the first time the DC multiple universe theme which was used constantly thereafter. But in the end it's nostalgia that drives the collectors and readers back to THE FLASH. The baby boomer generation has always carried a special place in their heart for the fastest man alive and, if history is any judge, so will future generations.

Historical Value	NEAR MINT- 9.2	
1970	1985	2004
$15	$900	$14,000

PLASTIC MAN (No. 1)

The career and character of comic book artist Jack Cole and his most famous superhero Plastic Man are intertwined. Never before in the Golden Age had a superhero character as original as Plastic Man been developed. With his ability to transform his body into any shape, Eel O'Brian could assume any number of configurations as he fought crime. It occurred to readers right away that this character was also a parody of the superhero idea in comics, and the fluid, wild inking style of Cole encouraged this interpretation. When Cole would design his pages, he would change panel shapes and sizes to fit the motion or changes Plastic Man was going through. Comic books fans loved the unexpected plot twists, the zany sense of humor, and the funny exchanges that eventually developed between "Plas" and his side-kick Woozy Winks.

PLASTIC MAN nn (No. 1) appeared on the stands in the summer of 1943 after the character had been featured in POLICE COMICS on a regular basis since 1941. The early Golden Age covers featured "Plas" in the shape of a bull's-eye, a giant balloon in a parade, as a bolt of lightning, or in the shape of a diamond on a football field about to confront a criminal team armed with bats, broken bottles, knives and other un-sportsmanlike devices.

Cole grew up in New Castle, Pennsylvania, and started his career in cartooning when he sold one-page fillers to Harry Chesler in 1938. By 1941 he had joined the Quality Comics Group and emerged shortly thereafter with his classic character. Cole would go on after Plastic Man to illustrate a number of *Men's Digest* magazines for the *Humorama* line. These simple wash cartoons, with their gorgeous women, paved the way for Hugh Hefner to take notice of Cole and ask him to come and work for *Playboy* magazine. A series of full page and full color cartoons soon began to grace the pages of *Playboy* and

Cole was an immediate favorite with his new audience. Though his previous black and white wash cartoons were used quite often for the covers on the *Humorama* digests, he never drew a *Playboy* cover, although he was featured on the *Playboy Cartoon* annuals that were later issued.

Cole also started his own syndicated strip entitled "Betsy and Me," and although he was at the height of his popularity and pay scale at *Playboy* and just forty-three years old, he took his own life in 1958 for reasons still unknown. He will always be remembered for the Golden Age character Plastic Man, who twisted and wound his way through comic book history, and whom without we would not have today a Mr. Fantastic of THE FANTASTIC FOUR.

Historical Value NEAR MINT- 9.2		
1970	1985	2004
$35	$60	$6,000

THE INCREDIBLE HULK No. 1

Jack Kirby had been with Stan Lee and Marvel Comics for several years when the "Marvel Age of Comics" began in 1961, but his output from 1958 through 1960 was concerned almost completely with what historians now call the "Pre-Hero" Marvel Comics. But this label doesn't really describe the Marvel Fantasy titles well. Most of the Atlas horror titles of the 1950s went down with the advent of the Comics Code Authority in 1954/55 while some like STRANGE TALES and JOURNEY INTO MYSTERY continued but were filled with watered-down science fiction and fantasy stories. By 1959 two new titles were added, TALES OF SUSPENSE and TALES TO ASTONISH, and from Jack Kirby, Dick Ayers, Steve Ditko, Joe Sinnott, Don Heck, Larry Lieber, and others an era of "Big Foot" Monster and Fantasy stories were introduced to readers that still have a charm of their own today. Many of the early concepts for Marvel's Silver Age superheroes were experimented with in these fantasy stories and the very name of "The Hulk" was used during this period of time, but for a white-furred space alien later renamed "Xemnu."

Unlike Spider-Man, the Fantastic Four, or especially the Avengers, the Incredible Hulk at first seemed to be a throw-back to the Marvel Fantasy and Pre-Hero comic days. As Bruce Banner staggered and raged and bellowed his way through the first few issues of THE INCREDIBLE HULK, he seemed to belong back in a pre-hero fantasy monster story, rather than a Marvel character of 1962. The artwork pencilled by Jack Kirby and inked by Dick Ayers also brought out this "monstrous" feeling, but actually what was happening was a novel concept within the superhero universe that would have a lasting effect. The Hulk actually had a lot in common with the Golden Age Sub-Mariner who also couldn't be trusted or considered as a superhero for a number of issues starting when he debuted in MARVEL MYSTERY COMICS.

Like Sub-Mariner, the Hulk was given to sudden rages and bitter reactions from the events in his life. However, what Stan Lee had really tapped into was the subconscious mind that lay beneath all human character, and as Bruce Banner developed so did the Hulk. From May of 1962 to March of 1963 there were only six initial issues of THE INCREDIBLE HULK. But after cancellation of his first title, the Hulk joined THE AVENGERS, made guest appearances in THE FANTASTIC FOUR, and finally found a home in TALES TO ASTONISH which would later evolve into THE INCREDIBLE HULK series two. The Hulk would eventually become one of the most popular of all Marvel characters; after all, he was way ahead of his time, and way ahead of the Terminator, the Punisher, Sylvester Stallone, Conan of the movies, and a host of other bigger-than-life tough-guys! He was, all in all, an original character, even if he was born of a prior era.

Historical Value	NEAR MINT- 9.2	
1970	1985	2004
$20	$750	$24,000

BATMAN THE DARK KNIGHT RETURNS

The publication of Frank Miller's landmark revisioning of Gotham City's favorite hero in a four part mini-series in 1986 was possibly the third most important and influential event in Batman's entire comic book career to date, after Bob Kane's introduction of the character in 1939 and the introduction of perennial sidekick Robin in 1940. Now the previous statement may seem like sacrilege to fans of such popular Batman artists as Neal Adams or Marshall Rogers, but those exceptionally talented Caped Crusader chroniclers who took the Batman back to his detective roots did not have half of the chutzpah that Miller did when he turned the Batman mythos upside down. Who else dared to fix up Harvey Dent, introduce a female Robin (why did this clever idea escape prior writers?), kill off the Joker AND faithful butler Alfred...permanently, make Selina Kyle fat, give Superman/Clark Kent a new and different twist, and, most incredibly of all, make the Batman OLD! Miller took the tired old DC chestnut of the "what if?" Batman tale and put real bite into it. Unlike the imaginary stories of the 1950s, when drama unfolded in Miller's tale, it was visceral, and most importantly, believable. Miller's deeply personal artistic style was the icing on the cake, giving comic panel blood loss a frightening reality.

The Dark Knight saga marked the end of a roughly 15-year era of Batman's career that was inaugurated when Neal Adams effectively killed the "camp" era in 1970. All of what Batman has become in the years since Miller's story can be directly traced back to him. Not only that, but the look and writing style of modern comics in general owes much to Miller's work, with its ultra-violent tone and nihilistic viewpoint. Add to this the fact that it is extremely unlikely that the lucrative Batman movie franchise, begun with Tim Burton's blockbuster 1989 film, would have ever been developed in the absence of Miller's tale, and you have more reasons to consider THE DARK KNIGHT RETURNS a great comic that can comfortably fit into a utility belt.

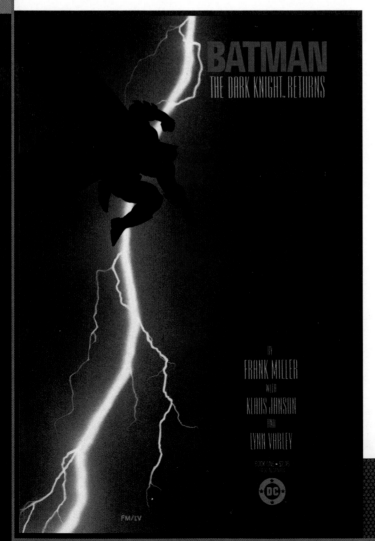

The Warner Books collection of the four part mini-series is chosen to represent Miller's work as the series really needs to be read in total to be properly appreciated, and this collection, released in both hardcover and paperback, gave a respectability to the comic form that was hitherto lacking. This book paved the way for the modern paperback and graphic novel collections so prevalent on the shelves of bookstores today.

Historical Value	NEAR MINT- 9.2	
1970	1985	2004
$0	$0	$10

KATY KEENE COMICS No. 1

KATY KEENE COMICS were unique, and as true to life as any comic book on the stands during the 1950s. Katy was created from the gifted pen of Bill Woggon, who had a style not too far removed from the Golden Age Wonder Woman artist H. G. Peter. Both Peter and Woggon drew their characters with a bold clear linear style, and they managed to portray women who were strong and powerful while at the same time being quite beautiful. Woggon developed his character for MLJ, and Katy first appeared in the Archie spin-off title WILBER No. 5, in the summer of 1945. Katy became a regular feature and quickly developed into a comic character where the readers could directly express their interest beyond the standard letters of comment. Here was a character for which they were asked to invent the clothing that Katy would wear from issue to issue!

By the mid-1940s comics publishers were beginning to see the first signs that, with the end of World War II, the superhero characters were encountering lowering sales figures. The advent of the crime comics, CLASSICS ILLUSTRATED, the Western comic books and the continuous advance in sales for WALT DISNEY'S COMICS & STORIES only reinforced that the market was evolving, and new ideas and characters could and should be introduced to readers. Katy Keene would also appear in MLJ's popular LAUGH COMICS (beginning in issue No. 20), PEP COMICS (appearing first in March of 1947), and SUZIE COMICS (beginning with issue No. 56), so she was fully developed (ahem!), and very popular before being given her own title. Woggon hit upon a very real audience when he developed Katy Keene and within four years of her introduction MLJ finally gave Woggon his own title when KATY KEENE COMICS No. 1 hit the stands in the latter part of 1949. By this time a Katy-fandom was in full swing, and the sales figures began to climb as more and more young girls read and saved the comics, while designing their own clothing for their now favorite/best comic character. At their height Woggon's titles sold thousands of copies, including the popular KATY KEENE PIN-UP PARADE and ARCHIE GIANT SERIES annuals which fans loved. It's no surprise that some of the top designers in the fashion industry of today will admit to reading this comic book, and drawing and designing their first concepts for clothing as children when they were Katy Keene fans!

Historical Value	NEAR MINT- 9.2	
1970	1985	2004
$5	$250	$1,250

MAUS

The first installment of MAUS appeared in Art Spiegelman's RAW MAGAZINE on the inside back cover of the 1980, No. 2 issue. The small, 7" x 5" twenty-page supplement comic was printed in black and white with the announcement that read "This is the first part of a projected 200-250 page work-in-progress. Future chapters will appear in RAW, on an occasional basis, as they are completed." By 1986, Pantheon Books released a two volume hardcover boxed set that included over 280 pages of the extended and complete saga. Preceded in content only by "Prisoner on Hell Planet," a four-page story from SHORT ORDER COMICS No. 1 in 1973, Spiegelman's MAUS had almost no precedent in comics. Only Bernard Krigstein's unforgettable "The Master Race" from EC's IMPACT No. 1 could come close to dealing with the emotional and historical subject matter of the fate of the Jewish people in Europe during World War II under the Third Reich.

What Spiegelman was attempting to do, in each small installment or one chapter at a time, was to retell his father's life as told from father to son, and in doing so come to terms with the fate that had fallen upon Vladek Spiegelman. Art Spiegelman had already made his historical mark in the Underground Comix as an introspective and conceptual artist who constantly sought what was best from the medium. He was briefly co-editor with Bill Griffith of ARCADE, THE COMICS REVUE and by 1977, the Beiler Press had collected his best work in the stunning BREAKDOWNS, a hardcover book of comics. Shortly thereafter, he founded the New Wave magazine *Raw* with Francoise Mouly in New York City.

Spiegelman's traditional inking style was sparse, and based in part on previous book illustrators who were masters of block-print design. When he began to execute the original artwork for MAUS, he brought his own brush work and scale under further discipline and control. His credo: less is more. It is almost as if the telling of this story required the artist himself to restrain himself stylistically, so that the narrative and emotional content could assume a life of their own. When most people read comic books, they project their own fantasies upon the words and pictures. With MAUS, Spiegelman invited the reader to become lost in an ever-expanding horizon of historical and personal narrative. As the reader became lost in the story, they were drawn closer to the truth.

Much has been written about the visual genius of choosing mice for Jews and cats for Germans, and much more has been written about the intellectual implications of MAUS, but of all the 100 greatest comic books within this volume, if you only go out and seek one to read, it should be MAUS.

Historical Value NEAR MINT- 9.2		
1970	1985	2004
$0	$50	$250

THE SANDMAN No. 1

Imagine a writer who expresses parts of himself from authors as diverse as Dickens and Verne and Bradbury and Poe. Imagine a writer who can sing a visual song of wonder, fear, doubt, and instinct to the unknown. Imagine this writer growing up after the Golden Age, after EC Comics, after the grand Silver Age of comics, after the Underground Comix, and the new wave. Imagine then how hard the road to writing comics is with something new, fresh, with the sting of "now" in it, but also with the heart of all contained within its history before? Just imagine.

And as your imagination wanders, you find yourself in a rich, fully focused world: the world of Neil Gaiman, the world of "The Sandman." How to write comics that are new? Why not make it hard on yourself and return to the past, pick a character, and bring him forth re-born!

Gaiman has said that when he wanted to write comics he was given his first instruction from Alan Moore, who allowed him to read his comics' scripts. From Moore's introduction he developed a writing style that detailed each panel of the story, giving the artist backgrounds, personalities of characters, and the narrative: all panel by painstaking panel! Gaiman would write specific stories for specific artists, stating that he had to know who would illustrate, before he could proceed with the script. This approach differed from many traditional writers like Harvey Kurtzman, who would draw cartoon panel pages with specific designs for each panel, to be delivered along with his scripts. By sticking to a literate written description for a specific artist, Gaiman was able to express himself fully while at the same time allowing his artists the creative freedom to express his ideas in their style. It's also important to remember that after the introduction and success of the Sandman, an entire publishing line (Vertigo Comics) was created and marketed, all because of the popularity and success of Gaiman's style of writing.

With this new found and focused writing style, Gaiman wrote a series of short stories scripted into comic book form and developed his own mythology for the Sandman. Contemporary times called for contemporary solutions, and as the 75 original comic books unfolded the public was introduced to Morpheus the modern Sandman, through the artwork of Mike Dringenberg, Malcolm Jones III, Kelly Jones, Craig Russell, George Pratt, and Sam Kieth. Comic book readers were stunned by what they encountered and they were drawn in by the finest writing in mainstream comics they had ever encountered. Today an entire fandom has formed around Gaiman's comic writing, and he has managed to flip over the previous "star" system in comics where titles were bought because of who illustrated them; now they buy a comic based on if Gaiman wrote it!

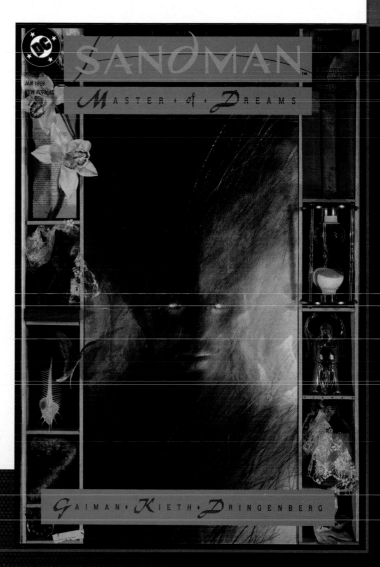

Historical Value NEAR MINT- 9.2		
1970	1985	2004
$0	$0	$40

NICK FURY AGENT OF S.H.I.E.L.D. No. 1

In 1968, readers were stunned by a compellingly different approach to comics' narrative with the first issue of NICK FURY: AGENT OF S.H.I.E.L.D. Introduced in STRANGE TALES 135 as imitation 007-type fare, Fury was transformed from a cigar-chomping dogface into the lethal high-tech warrior pitted against a league of international super-assassins. The real change, however, was not his substance, but his style. Fury thrillers became a graphic tour de force of cinematic technique employing dynamic symmetry, visual metaphors, symbolic montages, point-of-view angle shots, and match-dissolve transitions. Fans quickly learned to associate the new direction with the man who enigmatically signed his work with one name: Steranko.

A musician, fire-eater, ad agency art director, magician, male model, and master of other eclectic vocations, Steranko began his comics career after Captain America co-creator Joe Simon asked him to develop new characters to compete with Marvel. He created five one hour later and Simon selected three, resulting in Harvey's 1965 publication of Spyman, Magicmaster, and The Gladiator. Dissatisfied with their handling, Steranko bailed and subsequently sold another character to Paramount Pictures as a Saturday-morning TV series.

The same day, minutes before closing, he decided to visit Marvel and muscled his way past the receptionist into Stan Lee's office. They hit it off immediately. Lee shuffled through samples and said the work was crude, but it had something he liked: Raw energy! "What would you like to do for us?" Lee said, pointing to a tack of the month's comics. "Pick one!"

Steranko pointed to STRANGE TALES, which featured S.H.I.E.L.D., Marvel's rock-bottom effort. He figured that on this strip, there was nowhere to go but up! Never having drawn a single comic book, he was hired by Lee on the spot.

As a cautionary measure, Kirby laid out the first few issues to be finished and inked, but during the process, Steranko experienced a wave of discomfort he was unable to explain. He thought of himself as Kirby's biggest fan and reveled in their collaboration. So, when the concern grew to anguished proportions, he deconstructed the work intellectually and became aware of something about himself he hadn't known previously: that Kirby's storytelling philosophy and his were radically dissimilar.

After the shock of realization abated, he was on his own and put Fury through eighteen STRANGE TALES issues, until the strip was strong enough to warrant its own title. The series introduced other art forms – including surrealism, op-art, and expressionism – and such revolutionary graphic techniques as line-resolution photomontages, psychedelic color, strobe effects, and wild concepts such as a ten-issue serial that climaxed in a four-page spread that readers had to buy two issues to see all at once.

Steranko had arrived and comics would never be the same!

Historical Value NEAR MINT- 9.2		
1970	1985	2004
$1	$5	$200

ADVENTURE COMICS NO. 247

ADVENTURE COMICS No. 247 with its dramatic Superboy and Legion cover was a high water mark in the early Silver Age for DC Comics when it was released in March of 1958. The Legion of Superheroes was similar to the Green Lantern Corps that DC later developed in the Silver Age GREEN LANTERN title in that they all had their origins on other worlds and therefore were humanoid aliens.

The 1958 Legion Club that Superboy was asked to join in ADVENTURE No. 247 consisted of Cosmic Boy (Rokk Krinn who held the super-power to attract or repel metal based matter), Saturn Girl (Imra Ardeen who possessed advanced telepathic powers), and Lightning Boy (who later became Lighting Lad). However, by ADVENTURE #300 both Duplicate Girl and Mon-el had also been added to the Legion.

Curt Swan and George Klein did the cover artwork for most of the early Legion appearances, and Swan was at the time one of the most popular and successful of all DC artists, with his work gracing the covers for ADVENTURE COMICS for a number of years. The original appearance of the Legion of Superheroes was planned as a one-shot, but reader popularity brought them back issue after issue for a long series of adventures.

Eventually the Legion was reformed, and to this day the following members have been active at one time or another: Apparition (Tinya Wazzo), Brainiac 5.1 (a descent of Brainiac, who used force fields in his appearances), Ferro (who can change himself into iron), The Invisible Kid (a scientist who used his knowledge to gain invisibility), Kinetix (Zoe Saugin), Sister Andromeda (who gains her powers from a yellow sun), Star Boy (who can increase mass in other beings or objects), and a host of other interesting and complex personalities. The Legion has also been instrumental in a series of stories where their original history was erased. The event was named "Zero Hour" and thus their evolving history has continued to change over the years. High grade copies of ADVENTURE COMICS No. 247 are almost non-existent because the comic came out in 1958 when DC superhero comics were at their all time low print run in numbers, and almost none were saved as file copies.

Historical Value NEAR MINT- 9.2		
1970	1985	2004
$10	$750	$7,500

THE INCREDIBLE HULK No. 181

When writer Len Wein introduced the character of Wolverine in the pages of THE INCREDIBLE HULK No. 181 (with a cameo last panel appearance in the prior issue), he made him short in stature and in temperament, Canadian, and most importantly… a mutant. At the time, Wein was working on a proposed revival of Marvel's mutant heroes, the X-Men, and thought that Wolverine might be useful in revamping of the group. He had no idea how useful this little mutant could be.

Wolverine's first appearances in the final three months of 1974 were followed by GIANT SIZE X-MEN No. 1 in the summer of 1975. From then on, Wolverine's star would rapidly ascend in the comic world until he became the most popular member of the New X-Men, the most popular X-Man ever, and perhaps even the most popular comic character, surpassing Spider-Man, Batman, and Superman in the eyes of fandom for a period of time. During the short duration of his rise to stardom, Wolverine succumbed to the dark side of comics, becoming seemingly more bitter, angry, and vengeance filled with every appearance. He became, along with the Punisher and Frank Miller's Batman, the standard for the gritty and violent comic anti-heroes who spawned a host of imitators and influenced the way comics would be told and sold for a generation. It's no coincidence that Miller also helmed Wolverine's first solo title (a miniseries) and added even more *bête noire* to the mix.

The most important effect of Wolverine's popularity was his predominant contribution to the metoric rise of the X-Men, who nearly co-opted the entire Marvel Universe into their service. Marvel's REAL Mutant Agenda? Put mutants in every comic and see sales go up! Would Marvel have had such phenomenal success with The X-Men from the 1970s to today, and retain its leadership in the comics market, if Wolverine had not been part of the team? We will never know, but all evidence points to the feisty Canadian hero as being the cornerstone of almost 30 years of Marvel's success!

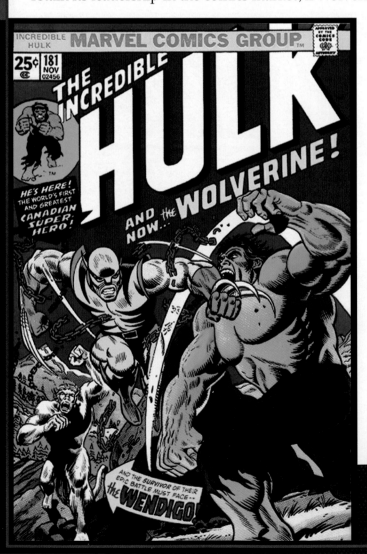

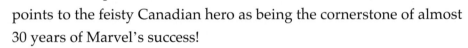

Historical Value NEAR MINT- 9.2		
1970	1985	2004
$0	$30	$2,250

WATCHMEN No. 1 was like no other series put out by a major comic company before. Action? Not really. Pin-up pages of heroes in action? Not a one. Trite tissue thin plots rehashed from a thousand other books? None. Literate? Yep.

The idea of the "literate comic" goes back as far as Gilberton's CLASSIC ILLUSTRATED series, but they cheated a bit as their stories were penned by such writers as Robert Louis Stevenson and Mark Twain, decidedly non-comic book professionals. The first inkling of what a well-thought mix of quality comic art and good storytelling could produce was brought to light by the EC line with their very literate titles, especially TWO-FISTED TALES and FRONTLINE COMBAT, both the children of Harvey Kurtzman. Unfortunately, just as the value of a well-written comic book was beginning to be appreciated, along came the Comic Code Authority which promptly squashed the freedom of speech that was necessary to tell an adult story in the four-color medium.

For nearly 30 years, the only "literate" comics were the comix (the undergrounds of the 1960s and 1970s), but these were available to a limited audience, were mixed in artistic merit, and all too often equated large doses of sex as being necessary for "adult" stories. It was not until the mid-1980s that the major comic companies finally allowed and even encourage experimentation in the adult vein. Perhaps spurred on by the phenomenal success of Art Spiegelman's MAUS, writers and artists were finally given a venue to present "adult" stories in the mass marketplace. It quickly became apparent that one of the best at doing "adult" literate stories in the comic medium was Alan Moore.

With WATCHMEN No. 1, Moore and artist Dave Gibbons created a world of over-the-hill heroes with very real problems. And they did it in a way that avoided the clichés of the superhero genre and captured the reader's interest. From the very cover of the first issue, with its bloody smiley face, the reader knew that this was no ordinary superhero comic. Over the course of 12 issues, Moore and Gibbons showed that a comic can be literate without being boring, and doing that in the superhero genre is doubly impressive. Comics turned a corner with the WATCHMEN miniseries and have never looked back. Sure, there are many titles that still rely on 20 pages of pin-ups to fill a book, but the number of books that have followed in the footsteps of WATCHMEN is encouraging: SANDMAN, and Moore's own SWAMP THING and V FOR VENDETTA are but a few examples. Literature finally triumphed over the Comics Code; it just took 30 years to do it.

WATCHMEN
No 1 of 12 $1.50 $2.10/CAN

SEPTEMBER 1986

Historical Value	NEAR MINT- 9.2	
1970	1985	2004
$0	$0	$10

THE SWAMP THING No. 1

"It walked in the woods. It was never born. It existed." With these few sentences science fiction and fantasy author Ted Sturgeon introduced to the world one of the finest and most original short stories, "It," published in John W. Campbell's UNKNOWN in August 1940. Sturgeon had no idea that he had brought to life a new Frankenstein (metaphorically speaking!) and a character that would appear and re-appear in the comics in a number of different transmutations starting with the Heap (appearing in AIR-BOY COMICS). Harvey Kurtzman's masterful satire of the Heap appeared in MAD No. 5 "Outer Sanctum!" and Marvel's THE MAN-THING all owe their existence to Sturgeon's original concept.

But it would take the combined writing talents of Joe Orlando (a veteran of the original EC staff who illustrated many stories for THE HAUNT OF FEAR, THE VAULT OF HORROR, and TALES FROM THE CRYPT) Len Wein, and the artistic greatness of a young Berni Wrightson, to bring to comics the very best variation on Sturgeon's idea—THE SWAMP THING. Appearing first as a short story in HOUSE OF SECRETS No. 92 (now an extremely "hot" collectors item), with inking assists by Berni's friends Jeff Jones and Michael Kaluta, this new character became an immediate success and soon was given its own title. Wrightson credited EC horror comics in general and Graham "Ghastly" Ingels in particular as part of his inspiration. Also interesting to note is the fact that another EC connection occurred when DC Comics briefly hired MAD publisher Bill Gaines to advise it on its comics' line. The very first thing Gaines suggested was that DC remove all the cover banners and title boxes that cluttered up the lower front covers. Because of this advice, when THE SWAMP THING No. 1 came out, the powerful and wonderful cover artwork of Berni Wrightson was 100% clear of any unsightly overlay labels. Wrightson's covers stand heads above most other comics of their time for their excellence in inking and their classic look of a 1950s comic.

THE SWAMP THING was a superhero without any costume. Misunderstood, lacking an alter-ego, this frightening creature still sought to do good. Wrightson created a gothic atmosphere in his stories and it's now apparent that he was one of the first people to successfully combine the best elements of the horror comics with superheroes and give modern day comics readers something fresh and original. Sturgeon lived long enough to see what Wrightson had wrought. Sturgeon also lived long enough to see his original "It" adapted by Marvel Comics in SUPERNATURAL THRILLERS No. 1 with cover artwork by Jim Steranko and interiors by John Severin and Frank Giacoia.

Historical Value NEAR MINT- 9.2		
1970	1985	2004
$0	$10	$150

THE FABULOUS FURRY FREAK BROTHERS No. 1

The artist responsible for the Freak Brothers, Gilbert Shelton, can arguably be called the only underground cartoonist who matched sales and popularity with Robert Crumb during the late 1960s and early 1970s when the counter culture was in full bloom. Shelton began to draw when he was a teenager and started a cartoonists' club in high school. He studied at the University of Texas and, while there, was the editor for the UNIVERSITY OF TEXAS RANGER which included many of his early cartoons. While living in Austin, he published the first printing of FEDS N HEADS in 1968 (which featured the premier appearance of the Freak Brothers) and became friends with fellow cartoonist Jack Jackson (responsible for one of the first Underground Comix with GODNOSE in 1964). After meeting Dave Moriarty and Fred Todd, the four would soon move to San Francisco and become part of the thriving poster and comix scene. Shelton would form a partnership with Moriarty and Todd and they bought a used printing press and founded The Rip Off Press in San Francisco in 1969. The fact that the artist doing the creative work for a comic would also own a share of the publishing firm that printed and distributed that comic was a revolutionary step, the implications of which would reach all the way to New York and affect the mainstream comics publishers in ways not yet imagined in 1969.

Shelton brought an absolute abandon to his work, and he spent just as much time making fun of the hippie life style, and the foibles of younger people, as he did taking shots at the established political order and "straight" society. People would read his comic books and actually fall down upon the floor with laughter (many had forgotten that this was the original function of comics by the 1970s!). Why? Because Shelton, like another grand humorist of everyday life Jackie Gleason, stayed close to the common events that filled people's lives. His drawing style was simple, direct, and his three famous hippies, Fat Freddy, Freewheelin' Franklin, and Phineas Phreak, continued to court disaster, initiate chaos, and in general find new ways to tickle the funnybone of anyone living through those times.

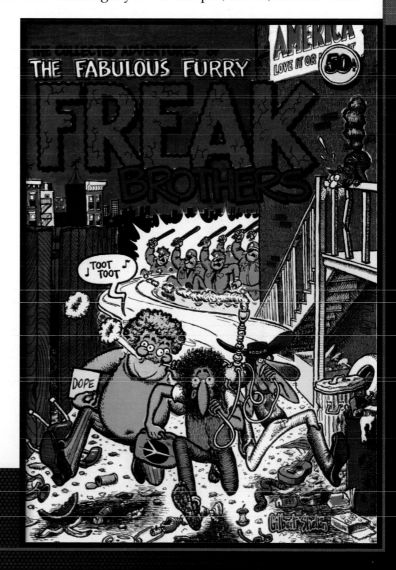

The very first printing (UG Comix, like the rock records of their time, would be released and if popular sent through several printings) of THE FABULOUS FURRY FREAK BROTHERS No. 1 can be identified by subtle printing differences on its cover. These differences include the tire leaning against the back wall is "grey," the cover price of 50 cents has a "purple" color, and other micro-scopically inane details! This comic in perfect condition is now worth $300, but you would gain much more pleasure from read-ing it than by having it contained in a CGC holder to obtain that certified high grade!

Historical Value NEAR MINT- 9.2		
1970	1985	2004
$0	$50	$300

The old adage that "you can't judge a book by its cover" might indeed apply to human beings, or books themselves, but it can hardly be applied to comic books. Within the comics industry you can not only judge a book by its cover, but you could pretty well be sure that the cover gave you an indication of what was waiting for you inside. Publishers knew how important covers were, and often hired the very best artists available to render striking covers for their comics, to the point that many 1940s Golden Age comic books contained remarkable covers and mediocre interior stories. By the 1950s, comic covers were perhaps even more important as the diversity in content of comics had begun to explode.

THE PHANTOM LADY No. 17, with its seductive and sexy cover by artist Matt Baker, is one of the greatest examples of its kind ever published. This book has stood the test of time, and has been kept in constant demand by the collectors and dealers who seek out good-girl comic books. Matt Baker began his career with the Iger studio in the 1940s and worked on a number of titles including SEVEN SEAS COMICS (where he illustrated Sea Girl), MOVIE COMICS (where he rendered Tiger Girl and Sky Girl), and eventually he even inked an entire issue of CLASSICS COMICS (No. 32 for LORNA DOONE) including the striking cover. Baker also worked for a period of time with Fiction House but he is best remembered for his work with Fox Publications for THE PHANTOM LADY. This title almost single-handedly created the "genre" name of good-girl art which comics' fandom attached to a number of books from the 1940s and 1950s. Baker's women were always stylish, very well drawn and proportioned, and they hosted the latest hair styles.

Tragically, Baker died just ten years after entering the comics industry, and very little is known about him today. What is known is that he was one of the first African-American comic book artists to work in the field, and his flair and style for

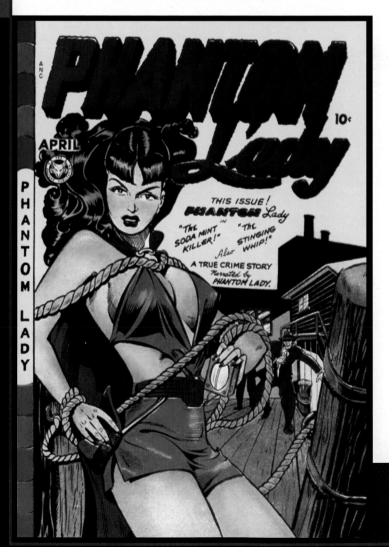

drawing women has earned him a permanent place in comics history. The cover for PHANTOM LADY No. 17 was given further fame when it was chosen by Frederick Wertham to be included in his book against comics *The Seduction of the Innocent*, where it was used as an example of how comics exploited women and sex. The quote accompanying the illustration read "Sexual stimulation by combining 'headlights' with the sadist's dream of tying up a woman." Wertham might be distressed to know that in today's market a Very Fine Plus condition of this comic book commands upward of $7,000! This all goes to prove you can sometimes judge a book by its cover and yes, that, Dr. Wertham, sex DOES sell!

Historical Value	NEAR MINT-	9.2
1970	1985	2004
$10	$900	$7,000

In the 1950s, when horror comic books were debuted by EC Comics' publisher Bill Gaines, it was apparent that a new best selling genre had been introduced into the comics industry. The previous crime comics of the late 1940s, such as CRIME AND PUNISHMENT and CRIME DOES NOT PAY, had already proven that very adult and extremely violent comic books could sell in the thousands. While EC was a very small publishing company (committed to quality, therefore sticking with its original three horror titles), other companies jumped on the band wagon early on and with a great number of titles. One such company was Atlas (previously called Timely and eventually Marvel Comics), and it entered the horror market in force. Titles such as JOURNEY INTO MYSTERY, STRANGE TALES, UNCANNY TALES, MYSTIC, ADVENTURES INTO TERROR, ADVENTURES INTO WEIRD WORLDS, ASTONISHING, JOURNEY INTO UNKNOWN WORLDS, MARVEL TALES (changed over from MARVEL MYSTERY), and SPELLBOUND, are just a small part of their total horror output!

STRANGE TALES was one of its first horror titles, first coming out in June of 1951. This title would outlast the horror era and outwit the Comics Code to survive well into its 100th issue of fantasy content, with the 101st issue debuting solo stories of the Human Torch in Marvel's Silver Age of comics. It would survive with the Human Torch, (Doctor Strange, and Nick Fury Agent of S.H.I.E.L.D.) well into its 168th issue and therefore ranks as one of the longest running Atlas/Marvel Comics while spanning three distinct eras.

The three eras are horror, pre-hero fantasy, and the superhero era; in each STRANGE TALES excelled. During the 1950s, many horror publishers equated more "gore" with more sales, and while EC strove to produce entertaining and excellently written and illustrated comics, many of its competitors did not. At Atlas however, there was quality, and beginning in the early issues of STRANGE TALES artists like Russ Heath, Bernard Krigstein, Gene Colan, and Joe Maneely turned in horror stories and covers that were excellent. During the pre-hero fantasy era STRANGE TALES enjoyed the work of Al Williamson, Jack Davis, Joe Sinnott, Steve Ditko, Jack Kirby/Dick Ayers, Gil Kane, Angelo Torres, Reed Crandall, and a host of other artists who turned in masterworks of fantasy. And then, again, in the superhero era STRANGE TALES was graced with the talents of Steve Ditko, Jack Kirby, Dick Ayers, Bill Everett, Jim Steranko, and John Severin. STRANGE TALES holds a special place in comics history, one it is not likely to relinquish anytime soon.

Historical Value NEAR MINT- 9.2		
1970	1985	2004
$15	$300	$4,000

ALL-NEGRO COMICS No. 1

When ALL-NEGRO COMICS No. 1 came out in June of 1947, an important milestone in the business of comics publishing had been reached. This 15-cent comic book contained a mix of stories and was brought into being by one Orrin C. Evans. Inside the front cover Mr. Evans proclaimed, in part, "Every brush stroke and pen line in the drawings on these pages are by Negro artists. Through Ace Harlem, we hope dramatically to point up the outstanding contributions of thousands of fearless, intelligent Negro police officers engaged in a constant fight against crime throughout the United States. Through Lion Man and Bubba, it is our hope to give American Negroes a reflection of their natural spirit of adventure and a finer appreciation of their African heritage." With Evans words, thousands of African Americans across the country would have rejoiced; unfortunately it's not certain that this important comic book received wide distribution outside the Philadelphia area.

Up until ALL-NEGRO COMICS No. 1 the presence of African-Americans in the comics was at best a mixed blessing and, all to often, a clear indication of just how much racism still plagued the United States. Yes, black characters were in the comics: THE YOUNG ALLIES had Whitewash (!); Will Eisner's popular THE SPIRIT had as his side-kick Ebony, CLASSICS COMICS had published "Uncle Tom's Cabin" (No. 15, November 1943); Walt Kelly had inked a series of covers for OUR GANG COMICS showcasing black children, and African Americans had appeared throughout the newspaper strip reprint titles and in other comics as background characters. But you had to stretch to find them. Moreover, there was not a single lead character certainly not a lead or secondary superhero to be found! Part of the intent of ALL-NEGRO COMICS was to challenge and to change these misconceptions.

Given time, ALL-NEGRO COMICS might have achieved its goals, but external forces made the first issue a one-shot. After the initial issue, publisher Evans' source for newsprint refused to sell to him, and he then was stonewalled by other suppliers in the Philadelphia area. There was no conclusive proof at the time to indicate whether the embargo was racially motivated or perhaps simply the common practice of larger publishers pulling strings to squash any new competitors. EC Comics would encounter similar back-biting during the 1950s Senate hearings on comics and the advent of the Comics Code Authority when a comic panel showing a black man sweating was deemed unpublishable. Whatever the motivations behind its blacklisting, the early demise of ALL-NEGRO COMICS was a sad ending to a noble venture. Decades later, comics are still struggling to portray minorities representatively and with dignity.

ALL-NEGRO COMICS No. 1 is now among the rarest of mid 1940s Golden Age comics, because of low distribution and for reasons unknown it is also almost never found in Fine or Mint condition. However, a copy CGC contained at Very Fine – 7.5 with off white pages recently sold at auction for $8,750.

Historical Value NEAR MINT- 9.2		
1970	1985	2004
$5	$400	$9,000

The origin and first appearance of Blackhawk by Chuck Cuidera with Will Eisner's assistance, along with the introduction of Jack Coles' The Death Patrol, and the Blue Tracer by Fred Guardineer, all appeared in the first issue of MILITARY COMICS in August of 1941. Just a few months before America's entry into World War II, this comic book which headlined itself as "Stories of the Army and Navy" can justifiably be called one of the first "War" comics, and the character that it introduced on the front cover, Blackhawk, would go on to outlive both his original publisher (Quality Comics Group) and the Golden Age itself.

Blackhawk was not the traditional patriotic hero fighting the axis during World War II, and the distinct quality of his team (they were not American, nor in the Armed Forces), along with its international ethnic make up, gave this comic character a unique opportunity to fight evil wherever it was found. Chuck Cuidera and Bob Powell worked together to create the Blackhawk concept, and they drew upon a number of different sources for their inspiration. They used the original concept being developed in Death Patrol (appearing in the same first issue) to begin their team, and they then expanded their idea using smart military style uniforms, the Grumman F5F fighter plane as the concept for the Blackhawk aircraft, and an international crew based upon a number of different popular personality types. Olaf was a typical Swede, Andre was a French Ronald Coleman, Chop-Chop was a classic stereotyped Chinese modeled after Milton Caniff's "Connie." and Hendrickson was a classic Dutchman. Chuck Cuidera did the entire artwork for the first eleven issues and then ironically was relieved of his command by the U.S. Military for service in World War II. Into the fold stepped a young man recently moved to New York from Newton, Kansas, named Reed Crandall. Somehow fate had delivered the right man to the right job, for Blackhawk and his team now began a series of stories and covers practically unmatched in the 1940s; this is not to say that the efforts of other artists such as Al Bryant, John Cassone, Dick Dillin, John Forte, Rudy Palais, and Bill Ward did not contribute to the Blackhawk legend! Blackhawk also enjoyed the writing talents of pulp and science fiction author Manley Wade Wellman, and pulp writer Joseph J. Millard.

Many forget that at his height in the mid-1940s Blackhawk was selling as many copies as CAPTAIN AMERICA and BATMAN, surely something to be proud of! Quality comics would eventually go under right after the 1950s horror comics crackdown brought down a number of publishers, and they sold out all their characters to DC Comics, except Blackhawk which was initially leased on a royalty basis but later bought outright. Because of this, and the fact that DC was keeping alive its last few remaining superhero titles from 1954 through 1959, Blackhawk escaped the Comics Code Authority and Golden Age guillotine that brought off the heads of all the other superhero titles.

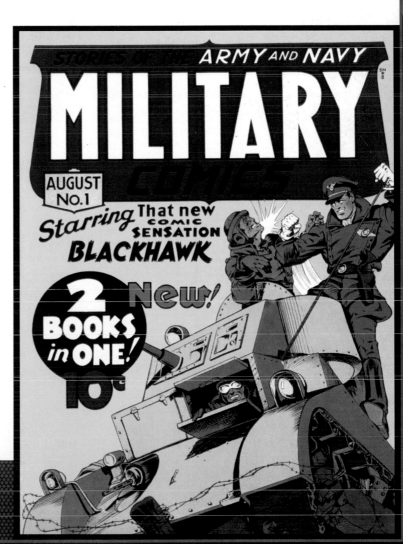

Historical Value NEAR MINT- 9.2		
1970	1985	2004
$80	$1,100	$12,000

POGO POSSUM NO. 1

Pogo was a newspaper strip character created by Walt Kelly originally for comic books in 1941. Pogo first appeared in ANIMAL COMICS No. 1. and then in Dell's FOUR-COLOR COMICS where he shared the bill with Albert the Alligator. Later, this small possum became one of the most popular newspaper strips and by the mid-1950s, he was read by thousands of Americans. With the Simon and Shuster softcover paper-back books going back to print time and again, magazine articles, and the occasional mention in the national press, could a comic book of his own be far behind? Artist Walt Kelly's characters exuded more emotional expression and contained more vitality than anything that had come before. Being able to draw and write and having also a "gift of gab," Kelly sustained the life and times of Pogo Possum throughout the 1950s.

When Dell Comics released FOUR-COLOR COMICS No. 105 in 1946, it featured the possum with the alligator in a double billing, but by the time that POGO POSSUM No. 1 hit the stands in October/December 1949, Pogo was the main character. Pogo became a cult favorite. The famous science fiction fan and author Lee Hoffman would constantly make references to Pogo in her fondly remembered 1950s fanzine *Quandry*. Walt Kelly could not keep up with both the demands of the newspaper strip and the comic books, so he found a reliable inker who worked for him in the 1950s, on both daily and Sunday sections as well as on the comic book work. This artist, Milton Story, has been lost to history, but he was an accomplished cartoonist. However, it was the same aforementioned power of Walt's pencils that allowed Milt to blend in perfectly, and the readers of the 1950s and today would never be able to guess which strips and comics were 100% Kelly and which were the result of this grand partnership!

Historical Value	NEAR MINT- 9.2	
1970	1985	2004
$10	$200	$1,000

SUPERBOY No. 1

When most leading superheroes were acquiring side-kicks, Superman remained a solo act. His charac-ter remained relatively untouched for a number of years. However, with MORE FUN No. 101 in January/February 1945, Superboy was introduced and continued to run in this title until its demise with issue No. 127 for November/December 1947.

SUPERBOY No. 1 hit the stands for March/April 1949, just 1 and 1/2 years later. DC had decided to expand the Superman character, and it chose to go back into Superman's youth, rather than create a new character. The approach had worked in MORE FUN, and it would work with SUPERBOY. Clark Kent's parents were well established in past references to Smallville, the town where he grew up. Smallville could slowly gain a life of its own, and the teen-age angle for Superman could be exploited.

Lana Lang became a high-school sweetheart in the new Smallville. Superboy struggled with his alter-ego Clark Kent, and his typical high school problems. Moreover, Superboy was constantly being accused of crimes or misdoings that he didn't commit. This was a very paranoid little town, and Clark Kent must have been ready to hit the road and leave for a metropolis to become a reporter when the time came!

The title SUPERBOY proved that the Superman family could be extended successfully, and as the years wore on, the family would continue to grow and prosper with additions of Supergirl and Krypto.

Historical Value	NEAR MINT- 9.2	
1970	1985	2004
$30	$1,200	$9,000

THE AVENGERS No.4

When THE AVENGERS No. 1 appeared in September 1963, it seemed as if Stan Lee at Marvel was playing catch up with Julius Schwartz over at DC and using newly created Marvel Silver Age characters for a new team-up comic title. The assembled team could not have been more different from the Justice League of America, the characters of which were much more dignified and adult in their bearing, and for readers of Marvel Comics, this team was not only fun and believable within the Marvel superhero universe, but also immediately popular.

The Avengers would evolve to become the backbone of Marvel titles, lasting over 400 issues and several annuals. THE AVENGERS No. 4 gave comic fans a milestone when they picked it up and saw Captain America running directly out of the cover! This important early timely Golden Age character was long overdue for a revival and given the attempt that Atlas (Marvel in the 1950s) made at keeping Captain America alive, it's a wonder that Stan Lee didn't revive him sooner.

Published in March 1964, this issue featured cover artwork by Jack Kirby and Paul Reinman, and it remains one of the finest early Marvel Silver Age covers in high demand by collectors and dealers alike. The original artwork for this special cover is in a private collection, and if it were to surface today at auction, it would easily sell for over $40,000! Captain America became an immediate and permanent member of the Avengers, and he played a major role in the action with issues 5 through 20. He was eventually given his own series in TALES OF SUSPENSE No. 58/59, and then eventually his own title with CAPTAIN AMERICA beginning with issue No. 100 (a continuation of the numbers of TALES OF SUSPENSE). CAPTAIN AMERICA had a long run with many Jack Kirby penciled covers for the early issues and a few spectacular Jim Steranko covers for issues 110, 111, and 113.

Historical Value NEAR MINT- 9.2		
1970	1985	2004
$5	$175	$2,500

109

DAREDEVIL No. 168

Frank Miller took over the artistic chords of DAREDEVIL at a critical juncture, for sales had been in a slump and even the return of perennial fan-favorite Gene Colan did not help. Miller's unique style caught the eyes of fans from the first issue he penciled (No. 158), but it was when his pencils and scripts were fused together that DAREDEVIL took off! Miller pumped new life into the character and helped invigorate what had been a sagging comic market.

Miller's first script for DAREDEVIL No. 168 contained a new female villain with a twist: she was a long-ago girlfriend of Matt Murdock, DD's alter-ego. Beginning with No. 168, the storyline careened into darkness and Miller never let up. Daredevil spent many of the next several years battling either Elektra or Bullseye, and having run-ins with Spider-Man's old enemy, the Kingpin of Crime, all the while trying to avoid homelessness, trying to help a friend with drug addiction, and having religious epiphanies (and all this was Comic Code approved!). Daredevil found himself involved in some truly grisly crimes, culminating with the impaling of Elektra on her own weapon by Bullseye in No. 181. Miller turned Daredevil's world into a relentlessly dark, oppressive, and tension-filled place. And it worked, for fans talked about a book that everyone had given up for dead. Frank Miller was the first savior superstar in comic history, but Miller was not a superstar when he saved DAREDEVIL: it *made* him one.

Historical Value NEAR MINT- 9.2		
1970	1985	2004
$0	$35	$75

THE AMAZING SPIDER-MAN No. 129

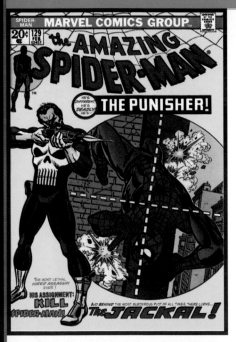

Other than Wolverine and the X-Men, no comics' character was as influential in 1980s and 1990s as the Punisher. He first appeared as a newly-minted villain in SPIDERMAN No. 129 (Feb 1974) and went on to greater glory as the first superstar anti-hero in comics.

Created by Gerry Conway, the Punisher derived his unique look from his costume's creator, legendary Spider-Man artist John Romita. Lured into battle against Spider-Man by the machinations of the Jackal, another seminal Spider-foe, the Punisher was clearly not a one-shot character. He quickly reappeared in SPIDER-MAN No. 134 and 135 in the same year, but was still every bit a man of mystery. His origin was published in 1975 in the pages of the black and white magazine MARVEL PREVIEW No. 2, no doubt because it was defined by the sort of violence that was forbidden by the Comics Code. For a period of about 10 years, appearances of the Punisher were eagerly awaited by fans. However, beginning about 1985, his appearances became so frequent that he often appeared to be in every single title Marvel published! By the mid-1990s, the character had descended into self-parody in THE PUNISHER MEETS ARCHIE and THE PUNISHER KILLS THE MARVEL UNIVERSE and, having been a victim of his own hype, had all four of his own series cancelled.

The Punisher was more than just another character in the Marvel universe. He was the basis of a new type of comic publishing theory that believed that there could never be too much of a good thing. For Marvel, this meant more Punisher, more X-Men, more Spider-Man, and less and less of everything else. In effect, the Punisher became less a character and more of a brand, to be relentlessly hyped on the comic buying public.

Historical Value	NEAR MINT- 9.2	
1970	1985	2004
$0	$5	$350

SHOWCASE No. 22   (PRESENTS GREEN LANTERN)

Considering that the Challengers of the Unknown, Lois Lane, and the Space Ranger, all of whom debuted right after SHOWCASE No. 4 with the Flash, were not traditional superhero characters, it's easy to see why comics readers were excited when the Silver Age Green Lantern first appeared in October/November 1959. This was still two years before the advent of THE FANTASTIC FOUR No. 1, and 2 and $1/2$ years before AMAZING FANTASY No. 15 appeared. Because DC still published the "original six" superhero titles that had survived the dark years of the late 1950s, and it was now re-introducing Golden Age superheroes in new forms, it was apparent that something special was taking place in comics.

The Golden Age Green Lantern had never really been assigned strong artists to illustrate his stories, but in the Silver Age, Gil Kane was given the assignment to illustrate the new Green Lantern and comics' fans were overjoyed. Kane's illustration style was elegant, his figures and backgrounds were strongly designed, and his ability to do knock-out covers was outstanding.

After three successive issues of SHOWCASE (Nos. 22-24), the character was given his own title when GREEN LANTERN No. 1 came out for July/August 1960. Not only did GREEN LANTERN now contain excellent artwork, but also the stories written by John Broome developed the his origins with more sophistication and gave readers plots that were interesting. After being gone from the newsstands for ten years, the Green Lantern was back.

Historical Value	NEAR MINT- 9.2	
1970	1985	2004
$10	$350	$6,000

MAGNUS ROBOT FIGHTER No. 1

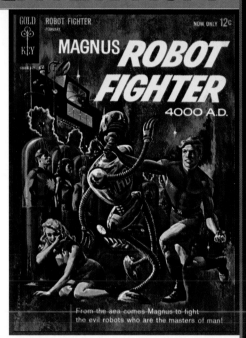

Russ Manning had already had a compelling career in comics before he began the first stories for Gold Key's highly popular science fiction title MAGNUS ROBOT FIGHTER. He was known for the elegant work he had done in TARZAN for "Brothers of the Spear," and had appeared throughout the late 1950s and early 1960s in a number of important Dell Comics titles including RAWHIDE, RICKY NELSON, WYATT EARP, BEN HUR, DALE EVANS, GENE AUTRY, and others. Manning had a style that was a cross between Burne Hogarth (with its swift and flowing natural figures in action) and Alex Raymond (with its towering architectural buildings and phenomenal interior designs) and there was really nothing that Manning could not render. Manning was given a full slate with MAGNUS ROBOT FIGHTER, where the world of the future included a city called North-Am that covered the entire American continent, where human beings were completely dependent upon robots for their every desire and protection, and where all of this technology had apparently advanced with loop-holes in the three laws of robotics (from Isaac Asimov's robot stories), the first and most important of which read…"A robot may not injure a human being, or, through inaction, allow a human being to come to harm."

In 4,000 A.D., a specially trained human appears, trained by a humanistic and concerned robot named 1A, who has seen the troubled waters that are about to rise against mankind and has trained Magnus in his early life to combat the problem. Magnus is equipped with special hearing devices so that he may intercept the speech wave voices of robots; he has steel smashing strength built into his hands and arms, and he has been taught every science known to man, but he is only a human being. Magnus began his quest in the heart of North-Am, where he immediately met and befriended Leeja the daughter of Senator Clane, and began his exciting contest against the mechanized age which would last 46 issues.

Historical Value NEAR MINT- 9.2		
1970	1985	2004
$5	$40	$300

FAWCETT MOVIE COMICS No. 15 (The Man From Planet X)

It was not until the 1950s that movie characters began to dominate the comics industry, an event brought about in part by the popular Western movie characters Gene Autry, Roy Rogers, and Hopalong Cassidy. The romance comics of the 1950s also tapped into the movie market, but sadly, there were too few 1950s horror and science fiction movies for there to be a wealth of comics adapted from this genre.

Ironically, there never were 1950s comic adaptations for *The Day the Earth Stood Still* (which would have become an instant classic), or other great films such as *Invasion of the Saucer-Men*, and *Forbidden Planet*. But three 1950s science fiction films that did see strong adaptations were *The Man from Planet X*, *When Worlds Collide*, featuring the excellent artwork of George Evans, and *Destination Moon*. All of these comics were from the popular, if short-lived series entitled FAWCETT MOVIE COMIC, which ran for twenty issues and featured mostly western movie titles in their other issues.

FAWCETT MOVIE COMIC No. 15, THE MAN FROM PLANET X, is a high water mark for 1950s comics. THE MAN FROM PLANET X is a masterpiece. The photo-cover was true to the movie and dramatic as anything that could be found on the newsstands in early 1952. The interior artwork by Kurt Schaffenberger and Robert Clark adapted the movie and characters very closely, while at the same time created an atmosphere of eerie suspenseful confrontation. It was a "first contact" story where human beings encounter an alien from another world. THE MAN FROM PLANET X is also another comic book that eludes collectors in high-grades; very few are known to exist in Near Mint condition. An excellent reprint was issued in 1987 that brought the comic back to fans in full original color, at a price people could afford.

Historical Value NEAR MINT- 9.2		
1970	1985	2004
$5	$700	$3,000

JOURNEY INTO MYSTERY No. 83

Stan Lee and Jack Kirby were trying to create a different kind of superhero when they began work on JOURNEY INTO MYSTERY No. 83, while incorporating already existing elements from other characters: Donald Blake's hammer, inscribed with the words: "Whosoever holds this hammer, if he be worthy, shall possess the power of …Thor!", was not too far removed from the original "green lantern" that had bestowed its power to Alan Scott, the original Green Lantern. The story behind Thor was also not that far removed from the mythological approach used for Wonder Woman. However, by the time that Joe Sinnott began to ink Kirby's pencils for THOR, it was apparent that Marvel had developed an entirely new and unique character, a god as a superhero.

Thor would become one of Marvel's most popular characters, and he carried the stylistic stamp of Jack Kirby's artwork with him into future issues. JOURNEY INTO MYSTERY was retitled THE MIGHTY THOR in 1966 (with issue No. 126) and by this time an entire world had been created around Asgard and the Norse gods. The intergalactic visual reach of Kirby's THE FANTASTIC FOUR also appeared within the pages of THOR as Donald Blake went to the ends of the universe to battle cosmic villains such as the colonizers, Ego the Living Planet, and Galactus.

The heroic figure in comics was never better portrayed, and as Marvel continued to unravel the stories, bombastic headlines like "The Stronger I Am, The Sooner I Die;" "The Living Planet;" and "To Become An Immortal," greeted fans. Using ancient mythologies to tell comic book stories brought out the very best in Jack Kirby's imagination, and today collectors are as delighted to own a page of original artwork from THOR inked by Vince Colletta as they are to own a page from THE FANTASTIC FOUR inked by Joe Sinnott. Many of these collectors consider Kirby's storytelling work for THOR to be the pinnacle of his career in comics.

Historical Value NEAR MINT- 9.2		
1970	1985	2004
$10	$500	$7,000

MISS FURY No. 1

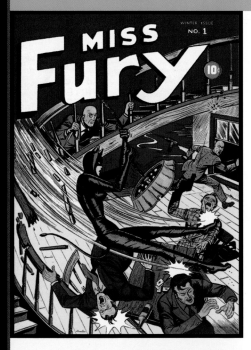

Miss Fury was the first newspaper strip and comic book female superhero character that was drawn and written by a woman, Tarpe' Mills. Tarpe' Mills had done comic book work as early as 1938, finishing stories for PRIZE COMICS, FAMOUS FUNNIES, and other early titles. She convinced the Bell syndicate in 1941 to begin her creation, Miss Fury, as both a daily and Sunday feature, and the world was introduced to one of the most original of all female superheroes (no small task in the male dominated world of newspaper syndicates). The Miss Fury, of the newspaper syndicate was a socialite, Marla Drake, who accidentally attended a costume ball, after learning that another woman planned on arriving with an identical outfit, in a panther skin left by her uncle. She never made it to the party, but instead started her career in crime fighting after meeting up with an escaped murderer.

Although Miss Fury didn't display her figure with a sexy costume in the same way as Wonder Woman, she was an incredible character and the newspaper strip introduced Detective Carey and a number of other important characters during its run. Timely Publications obtained the rights to bring Mills' character into comics when MISS FURY No. 1 was published in the winter of 1942-43. Running only eight issues, with cover and interior artwork by Mills, although Alex Schomburg did the cover artwork for issues Nos. 1, 5, and 6, the comic was composed of some of the best newspaper strip reprints. June Tarpe' Mills struggled and attained something no other woman had done in the 1940s, having created and drawn a female comic hero who became popular based on her character and actions, not her sex appeal or pin-up value, which is something many female superheroes of today cannot claim.

Historical Value NEAR MINT- 9.2		
1970	1985	2004
$50	$750	$5,000

OUR ARMY AT WAR No. 81

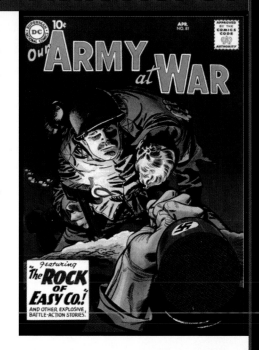

OUR ARMY AT WAR No. 81 was for many years one of the most obscure of all comics published in the 1950s. But as the 1960s and 1970s unfolded, with the advent of comics fandom and *The Overstreet Comic Book Price Guide*, things began to change. Every collector became aware of comic history, and OUR ARMY AT WAR No. 81 now has its place firmly attached in that history and is therefore on many a comic want list.

OUR ARMY AT WAR No. 81 presents the proto-type of the Sgt. Rock character, which would not be fully developed until issue No. 83. The No. 81 artwork by Ross Andru and Mike Esposito had enough positive reader response for Joe Kubert, Robert Kaniger, and Mort Drucker to fully develop Sgt. Rock two issues later. Sgt. Rock is the most famous and longest running character related to a war comic title. His popularity and strength in fandom are augmented by the artwork of two of DCs Comics' masters: Joe Kubert and Russ Heath. Both of these artists had careers in comics that began in the 1940s. Kubert started early in 1942 and eventually became a DC house artist. Russ Heath began his comic work in 1946 and quickly became employed by Timely/Atlas comics during the late 1940s and early 1950s. When these two artists were given the St. Rock stories to illustrate, their styles were fully matured, with Heath executing his masterful grey-tone comic covers for DC that are justifiably considered classics.

St. Rock was a tough, hard-love kind of character associated with war comics in the 1950s, but by the 1960s he became an experienced veteran, Easy Company (his battle unit) grew up, and Rock would eventually become a General! OUR ARMY AT WAR is the longest running continuous war comic beginning in August of 1952, and lasting 300 issues until February of 1977. The popularity and importance of OUR ARMY AT WAR No. 81 was recently reinforced when a Very Fine Plus copy (with bone white paper) recently surfaced, and was sold for nearly double Near Mint *Overstreet Guide* at $6,000!

Historical Value	NEAR MINT- 9.2	
1970	1985	2004
$1	$100	$7,500

TARZAN NO. 1

After the appearance of the LARGE FEATURE COMIC, the early SINGLE SERIES No. 20, and two individually released Tarzan comics by Dell in its FOUR-COLOR SERIES (Nos. 134 & 161), Dell Comics released TARZAN No. 1 for January/February of 1948. The cover and interior artwork were by Jesse Marsh, who had previously done the artwork for Dell's FOUR-COLOR JOHN CARTER OF MARS, and who would retain his position as primary artist on TARZAN until near the end of the Dell run. Burroughs' fans were at first unhappy with Dell's choice of artist, having been previously spoiled with the likes of Harold Foster and Burne Hogarth, but they soon came to appreciate the gentle and direct approach that Marsh brought to the Tarzan character. Marsh had worked previously for the Walt Disney Company from 1939 through the 1940s, and contributed work to *Pinocchio*, *Fantasia* and other Disney films. He began his work for Dell Comics in 1945 while still holding down his job at the Walt Disney Company, and contributed work to such titles as GENE AUTRY, and DAVY CROCKETT. Marsh would do both the cover and interior artwork for the first 12 issues of TARZAN, then Dell began a series of colorful photo-covers featuring Lex Barker who portrayed Tarzan on film. Beginning with issue No. 55, the first in a series of cover paintings by Morris Gollub, recognized by Burroughs' fans as having produced some of the finest TARZAN covers for this series, continued through issue No. 79 at which time the photo-covers reappeared.

TARZAN continued uninterrupted throughout the 1950s and then changed over from Dell to Gold Key Comics in the 1960s. It's important to also remember that Edgar Rice Burroughs lost personal control over his licensed creations in 1948 and died in 1950. Although the golden days of Tarzan's newspaper exploits were a thing of the past, the tradition that Burroughs had started in October of 1912 was carried on for a number of years by Jesse Marsh and a new generation of comic artists.

Historical Value	NEAR MINT- 9.2	
1970	1985	2004
$15	$300	$1,750

REFORM SCHOOL GIRL

For sheer audacity and exploitation, REFORM SCHOOL GIRL nn by of all publishers, Realistic Comics, stands as one of the all-time outstanding comic books. It's a wonder that retailers didn't take this comic right out of the string-tied bundles and burn it upon inspection! However, by 1951 when it was released their eyes had been thoroughly burned out by the previous crime comics and the newly released horror comic books that they were selling. What were kids (and the parents of any doomed child who was able to buy this comic book and bring it home) to deduce from the wild frizzy haired, cigarette smoking (stylish hanging sideways Marlon Brando-like), nylon stockings being pulled up, beautiful high school drop out (knock out) young woman? Frederick Wertham had a field day with this comic book in his *Seduction of the Innocent* when his byline quote read "Comic books are supposed to be like fairy tales." Wertham also complained that this comic blended "sex, violence, and torture in its context" and he was right! Here was a comic book printed in 1951 that violated every single family value imaginable, and it was sitting on the newsstands right beside WALT DISNEY'S COMICS & STORIES and ARCHIE COMICS.

Actually this comic book was a direct tie-in with the paperback book release of the same title, published by Diversity Publishing Company in Chicago, Illinois, in 1948. A popular Canadian professional skater named Marty Collins had posed for the cover (no doubt as a joke) when the paperback was released in 1948, and much to her dismay would have found her smaller book image spread across the newsstands in 1951. REFORM SCHOOL GIRL nn is today sought out by collectors of good-girl art, as well as those seeking the most outrageous teenage rebellion title of all time.

Historical Value NEAR MINT- 9.2		
1970	1985	2004
$10	$800	$3,000

CASPER THE FRIENDLY GHOST No. 1

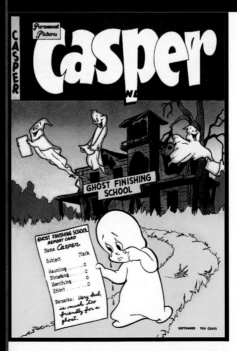

CASPER THE FRIENDLY GHOST No. 1 came out in September of 1949, published by the St. John Publishing Company. It was with this comic that the sentimental ghost who didn't want to scare anyone actually got his full name! Before the comic book, Casper had appeared in an animated cartoon released in 1945 by Paramount Pictures as part of its "Noveltoons" series. Created from a story written by Seymour Reit and Joe Oriolo, this first cartoon was popular enough to bring about a sequel entitled "There's Good Boos Tonight," released in 1948. More cartoons followed, and by 1949 St. John had secured the rights to publish the comic book.

The St. John title lasted only five issues, and the No. 1 copy is now quite scarce in higher grades because of low distribution. In 1952, the license was bought by Harvey Comics and Casper kicked into high gear with a long run sporting colorful covers. It was during his time in comics that Casper developed his family of the Ghostly Trio, and obtained a true friend with his ghost horse named Nightmare. The comic book publication of Casper far outlasted the animated cartoons and it was not until 1959 that animated cartoons began to appear again on TV with "Matty's Funday Funnies." When Harvey changed the title name with issue No. 70 from CASPER, THE FRIENDLY GHOST to THE FRIENDLY GHOST, CASPER they certainly caused some confusion for collectors!

By 1995, the release of the major movie *Casper, The Friendly Ghost*, directed by Brad Silberling and starring Bill Pullman, Christina Ricci, and Cathy Moriarty, with the animated character of Casper, brought the character back to life. Casper is remembered today as one of the most popular and successful of all humorous characters in the comics.

Historical Value NEAR MINT- 9.2		
1970	1985	2004
$4	$175	$2,000

SUPERMAN PEACE ON EARTH

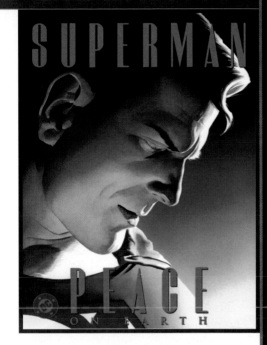

Alex Ross has helped to change the face of comics narrative history with an artistic style that is based in traditional approaches and with the gift of knowing when to stop a painting. This may sound like a strange way to describe the working methods of one of today's most popular comic artists, but comprehending the process by which Ross paints can lead to an understanding of why his work is so popular among readers. When Ross first appeared on the scene the direct market, the market for adult comics and products for comic special-ty stores, had for years been developing expensive, artistically creative, and lavishly produced comic books. Many of these titles catered to the reputation of the artist doing the book, and thus the vehicle for sales became the art, rather than the story.

As Ross began to develop his approach to comics, he used a traditional straight-forward style of painting. He freely admits, and credits in his books, using live models and photography to pose these people into posi-tions that he may use for specific panels within the story plot. By bringing a simple, direct, and restrained paint-ing style into comics, Ross managed a quiet revolution. All of a sudden, overworked, over-embellished, over-crowded, and visually confusing comic narratives were challenged by this back-to-the-basics Norman Rockwell style approach! It doesn't sound revolutionary, but it was, and when Charles Kochman, an editor at DC Comics, pushed for large format graphic novels for the new Alex Ross projects, the results were stupendous!

SUPERMAN PEACE ON EARTH is the perfect example of how Ross tells a story, and it will always be remembered for the emotional impact that it had on readers who came across it for the first time in the winter of 1999. Comics fans turned the pages, absorbed the beauty of the painted narrative, and returned to their favorite scenes, and they were reading a story and not just looking at beautiful art; after a long hiatus in comics, form was again following function.

Historical Value NEAR MINT- 9.2		
1970	1985	2004
$0	$0	$20

OUR GANG COMICS No. 1

The original "Our Gang" (known also as "The Little Rascals") made their film debut in 1922 as the cre-ation of movie director Hal Roach. Hal Roach Productions produced a great number of these episodes dur-ing the 1920s and these simple films had a magical and spontaneous energy that would be impossible to recreate in today's Hollywood. "Our Gang" had many members over the years, but the most popular were Jean Darling, Gordon "Porkey" Lee, George "Spanky" McFarland, Jackie Cooper (who played in only 15 episodes), Pete (the pit bull dog), Buckwheat, and Alfalfa. When Roach sold the rights to "Our Gang" to M.G.M in 1938, some of the magic went out of the filming, and they began to decline in popularity until their final episode was shot in 1944.

Nearly at the end of their career in film, Dell Publications decided to launch the comic book OUR GANG COMICS No. 1 for September of 1942. This first issue contained artwork by a young man who would exert a great influence on comics in the future: Walt Kelly. Kelly did the interior stories for OUR GANG, and began to do cover artwork as well, coming into his own stylistically with OUR GANG No. 10 onward, where he inked successive masterworks for the comics. Kelly's cover depictions of children were universal and charm-ing. Inside, Kelly was eventually joined by that other master of story telling, Carl Barks, when Carl began a series of stories revolving around Benny Burro, Barney Bear and Happy Hound.

OUR GANG COMICS lasted only 59 issues; ironically, the last two issues featured no "Our Gang" story or Kelly artwork and the book ended its run in 1949. But Kelly had been given the space and time to mature, and eventually POGO POSSUM would carry him to greater heights in the comic world.

Historical Value NEAR MINT- 9.2		
1970	1985	2004
$25	$400	$1,200

The Brownies, Their Book

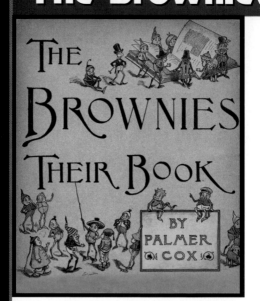

St. Nicholas Magazine, the first children's periodical, had debuted nine years before Palmer Cox's famous creations, The Brownies, took their first bow in its pages in 1883. Just four years later, Cox got the idea to put together a collection of previously published Brownies stories along with some new material in THE BROWNIES, THEIR BOOK (NO. 1). Its publication marks one of the most significant milestones in the history of the medium, ushering in the Platinum Age and defining the composition of comics for the next 50 years. A series of such books followed. Further, Cox achieved a significant degree of stature by licensing the characters to a wide variety of products, creating a thriving financial entity, a virtual roadmap used years later by Kay Kamen and Walt Disney when publicizing Mickey Mouse. Kodak's Brownie camera is perhaps the most famous of the licensed items produced, but it is only one of the many.

In one of *St. Nicholas Magazine*'s biographical sketches on Cox, writer Malcolm Douglas describes the Brownies as "a very strange little band of night-sprites; tiny, neckless creatures with big ears, pop-eyes, wide, smiling mouths, fat, round paunches, spindling legs, and long, tapering feet... queer little supernatural beings, with traits that irresistibly appealed to one's sense of the ridiculous."

With his painstakingly detailed illustrations and rhymed story-poems, Cox brought elements of wild imagination and the slightly absurd to the lives of 19th century children. His work clicked with the kids right away, since the Brownies suggest a group of characters that managed to outwit the adults they encountered. The Brownies quickly came to embody several distinct and separate personality types: the Irish Brownie (a tribute to America's burgeoning immigrant population), then the Policeman, then the Dude (Cox's personal favorite, representing sophisticated New Yorkers), the Cadet, the Chinaman and, later, the Cowboy (who emerged at the request of then-President Theodore Roosevelt).

Historical Value	NEAR MINT- 9.2	
1970	1985	2004
$15	$75	$3,000

CEREBUS THE AARDVARK No. 1

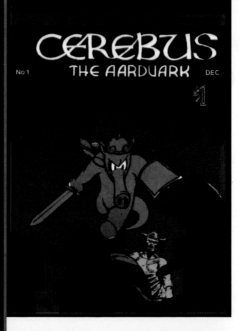

CEREBUS THE AARDVARK No. 1 was written, drawn, and printed by creator Dave Sim in Canada in December of 1977. This independently produced and distributed comic book has lasted for well over 200 issues and is still published today and the popularity and demand for back issues built to such a degree that large reprint square back annuals sold in the thousands during the 1980s. The impact of the success of CEREBUS on the market has been remarkable and the very existence of this comic book has made it possible for hundreds of individual independent efforts to come forth in the 1980s and 1990s.

Part of Sim's success has to do with the fact that the character Cerebus is a visual metaphor that allows the creator to take on a number of different comic book themes and look at them with a different angle. Sim has created an entire world and mythology around his small aardvark, one that is followed with just as much intensity by his fans as those who read and re-read the Tolkien trilogy.

The first printing of the first issue was only 2,000 copies, and many of these had printing defects. But the major difference between CEREBUS and the standard UG comix was that the content of CEREBUS was such that they were violent and suggestive of sex, but essentially refrained from the visual excesses of the UG comix. Therefore Sim began to build into his printing production a diverse and highly organized distribution network that was backed up by the advent of the direct comic market. The direct market expanded in the 1970s and 1980s and was built around the comic book specialty stores that sprang up all over America, at their height well over 6,000. It was these stores and the hard-core comics fans that frequented them that were the core of the CEREBUS success story.

Historical Value	NEAR MINT- 9.2	
1970	1985	2004
$0	$50	$350

Ask veteran comic book collectors to name one of the all-time great adventure, Edgar Rice Burroughs-related covers by a Golden Age legend and they will very quickly point to Lou Fine's effort for JUNGLE COMICS No. 1. This fantastic cover, printed for January of 1940, depicts Kaanga, Jungle Lord, swinging from a tree about to engage a lion in battle, while a beautiful young girl lays prone across the bottom of the scene. The cover follows famous pulp art collector Robert Lesser's rule that every great cover needs "A victim, a victor, and the vanquished!" This statement applied to 100% of the pulp magazines of the 1930s and it certainly did as well for the covers of JUNGLE COMICS!

Lou Fine was noted for greatness by comic book artists of the time, all whom worshiped the ground he trod upon (as he made his way to his drawing desk)! He was soon joined by Will Eisner, Bob Powell, Reed Crandall, Bob Lubbers, John Celardo, and Matt Baker, all of whom quickly made JUNGLE COMICS one of the most popular 1940s titles. Collectors now seek out issues with "bondage covers," and JUNGLE COMICS is notorious for its panels depicting negligees and torture, certainly all exploitation themes found in the comics of the 1940s.

JUNGLE COMICS was published by Fiction House, known for its pulp titles and PLANET COMICS. It was, besides Ziff Davis, the only pulp publisher to make a large commitment to printing comics in the 40's. Fiction House was attacked by both Fredric Wertham in his book *Seduction of the Innocent* and Geoffrey Wagner in *Parade of Pleasure* for being racist and misogynistic, a charge they were not wholly innocent of. Despite these cultural attacks, their titles continued to be popular with readers up until their demise in the summer of 1954.

Historical Value	NEAR MINT- 9.2	
1970	1985	2004
$60	$400	$6,000

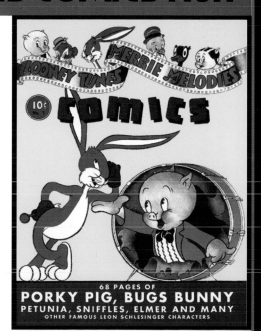

The only other major competition for the Walt Disney Company in the 1940s comics market was the Warner Brothers cartoon characters. Beginning with LOONEY TUNES AND MERRIE MELODIES COMICS No. 1 in the Fall of 1941, Bugs Bunny, Daffy Duck, Elmer Fudd, Porky Pig, and a host of other Warner characters descended onto the comic book pages. In the same year Warner Brothers' cartoon department had firmly established itself with Leon Schlesinger productions. Tex Avery began his career with Schlesinger and was responsible for creating Bugs Bunny while Joe Dougherty and Mel Blanc became the recognizable voices for Porky Pig's "sss-ttt-u-tt-errrrr-ing" voice. Warner cartoons were giving Disney a run for his money!

The comic book adaptations of Schlesinger cartoon characters began with an early newspaper strip entitled BOSKO, but it was not until LOONEY TUNES AND MERRIE MELODIES COMICS came out that their popularity with comic readers began to expand. During the 1950s, Warner characters were everywhere as Western Color (Dell Comics) expanded into many different titles with BUGS BUNNY, DAFFY DUCK and PORKY PIG being among the top sellers.

During the 1940s, Bugs Bunny and Porky Pig shared the cover for the first 50 issues with the exceptions of Nos. 19, 22, 26, 29, 30, 45, 49, and 50, where either Bugs or Porky appeared by themselves. LOONEY TUNES AND MERRIE MELODIES COMICS also enjoyed the talents of artist Walt Kelly for a number of issues when he illustrated the Super Rabbit stories. Super Rabbit holds the title for the first funny animal superhero and appeared as early as issue No. 5.

Historical Value	NEAR MINT- 9.2	
1970	1985	2004
$50	$500	$12,000

Title	1970	1985	2004
1.) ACTION COMICS 1	500.	15,000.	500,000.
2.) FUNNIES ON PARADE nn	125.	715.	17,000.
3.) SUPERMAN 1	350.	11,000.	300,000.
4.) NEW FUN COMICS 1	100.	1,200.	55,000.
5.) MAD 1	30.	400.	14,000.
6.) MICKEY MOUSE MAG 1	125.	600.	17,500.
7.) ZAP COMICS 1	25.	250.	4,000
8.) MARVEL COMICS 1	350.	16,000.	275,000.
9.) WHIZ COMICS 2	250.	8,000.	75,000.
10.) BATMAN 1	175.	5,000	125,000.
11.) WALT DISNEY'S 1	115.	3,000.	30,000.
12.) AMAZING FANTASY 15	30.	2,000.	60,000.
13.) DETECTIVE COMICS 38	60.	1,800.	55,000.
14.) ALL-STAR 3	135.	2,250.	75,000.
15.) CAPTAIN AMERICA 1	150.	5,500.	150,000.
16.) FAMOUS FUNNIES 1	125.	550.	27,000.
17.) CRYPT OF TERROR 17	35.	500.	10,000.
18.) DETECTIVE 1	125.	2,500.	75,000.
19.) ALL-STAR 8	50.	1,000.	44,000.
20.) SHOWCASE 4	15.	1,200.	45,000.
21.) ARCHIE COMICS 1	10.	1,000.	30,000.
22.) CLASSICS COMICS 1	1.	600.	8,000.
23.) DETECTIVE COMICS 27	375.	17,500.	500,000.
24.) PLANET COMICS 1	50.	1,250.	17,500.
25.) LONE RANGER nn	15.	200.	8,000.
26.) NEW YORK WORLD'S FAIR 1939	90.	1,000.	32,500.
27.) CAPTAIN MARVEL nn	125.	5,000	40,000.
28.) YOUNG ROMANCE 1	5.	50.	1,000.
29.) FOUR-COLOR COMICS 386	15.	500.	2,500.
30.) CRIME DOES NOT PAY 22	10.	700.	6,000.
31.) FOUR-COLOR COMICS 16	30.	1,750.	17,000.
32.) WEIRD SCIENCE 12 (1)	45.	600.	8,000.
33.) ALL-AMERICAN 16	70.	3,500.	150,000.
34.) MOTION PICTURE 1	5.	5,000.	27,000.
35.) FLASH COMICS 1	150.	3,500.	125,000.
36.) WALT DISNEY'S 31	15.	900.	4,500.
37.) FANTASTIC FOUR 48	1.	35.	1,500.
38.) VAULT OF HORROR 12	35.	700.	12,000.
39.) YOUNG ALLIES 1	50.	1,100.	22,000.
40.) GIANT SIZE X-MEN 1	.0	14.	1,300.
41.) PICTURE STORIES FROM THE BIBLE 1	3.	30.	600.
42.) SPIRIT WEEKLY 1	10.	500.	750.
43.) FOUR-COLOR 74 LULU	7.	400.	2,250.
44.) AMAZING SPIDER-MAN 1	20.	900.	50,000.
45.) JUMBO COMICS 1	80.	1,000	24,000.
46.) FOUR-COLOR nn D.T.	50.	500.	10,000.
47.) DONALD DUCK nn	75.	1,000.	5,000.
48.) FANTASTIC FOUR 1	25.	1,250.	50,000.
49.) SINGLE SERIES 20	100.	450.	2,500.
50.) GENE AUTRY 1	14.	450.	10,000

Title	1970	1985	2004
51.) BRAVE & BOLD 28	5.	350.	8,000.
52.) YELLOW KID M.F. 1	10.	250.	11,000.
53.) THE X-MEN 1	15.	450.	16,000.
54.) HIT COMICS 1	50.	900.	10,000.
55.) CONAN 1	.15	75.	350.
56.) WONDER WOMAN 1	50.	1,000.	34,000.
57.) 3-D COMICS TOR 1	12.	75.	250.
58.) THUNDA KING OF THE CONGO 1	30.	800.	2,500.
59.) CRIME SUSPENSTORIES 22	5.	75.	700.
60.) STRANGE ADV. 1	10.	400.	5,000.
61.) GREEN LANTERN 76	1.	75.	350.
62.) SHADOW COMICS 1	50.	500.	8,000.
63.) HOT ROD COMICS nn	1.	25.	450.
64.) THE FLASH 105	15.	900.	14,000.
65.) PLASTIC MAN 1	35.	600.	6,000.
66.) THE INCREDIBLE HULK 1	20.	750.	24,000.
67.) DARK KNIGHT 1	0.	0.	10.
68.) KATY KEENE COMICS 1	5.	250.	1,250.
69.) MAUS 1	0.	50.	250.
70.) THE SANDMAN 1	0.	0.	40.
71.) NICK FURY 1	1.	5.	200.
72.) ADVENTURE COMICS 247	10.	750.	7,500.
73.) THE INCREDIBLE HULK 181	0.	30.	2,250.
74.) THE WATCHMEN 1	0.	0.	10.
75.) THE SWAMP THING 1	0.	10.	150.
76.) FREAK BROTHERS 1	0.	50.	300.
77.) PHANTOM LADY 17	10.	900.	7,000.
78.) STRANGE TALES 1	15.	300.	4,000.
79.) ALL-NEGRO COMICS 1	5.	400.	9,000.
80.) MILITARY COMICS 1	80.	1,100.	12,000.
81.) POGO POSSUM 1	10.	200.	1,000.
82.) SUPERBOY 1	30.	1,200	9,000.
83.) THE AVENGERS 4	5.	175.	2,500.
84.) DAREDEVIL 168	0.	35.	75.
85.) THE AMAZING SPIDER-MAN 129	0.	5.	350.
86.) SHOWCASE 22	10.	350.	6,000.
87.) MAGNUS ROBOT FIGHTER 1	5.	40.	300.
88.) FAWCETT MOVIE COMICS 15	5.	700.	3,000.
89.) JOURNEY MYSTERY 83	10.	500.	7,000.
90.) MISS FURY 1	50.	750.	5,000.
91.) OUR ARMY AT WAR 81	1.	100.	7,500.
92.) TARZAN 1	15.	300.	1,750.
93.) REFORM SCHOOL nn	10.	800.	3,000.
94.) CASPER THE FRIENDLY GHOST 1	4.	175.	2,000.
95.) SUPERMAN PEACE ON EARTH	0.	0.	20.
96.) OUR GANG COMICS 1	25.	400.	1,200.
97.) THE BROWNIES, THEIR BOOK	15.	75.	3,000.
98.) CEREBUS THE AARDVARK 1	0.	50.	350.
99.) JUNGLE COMICS 1	60.	400.	6,000.
100.) LOONEY TUNES 1	50.	500.	12,000.

JERRY WEIST has been in comics as a fan, dealer, and professional since 1958. First publishing the groundbreaking *EC Squa Tront* in 1967 with Roger Hill and Bob Barrett, he developed life-long friendships with Bill Gaines, Al Feldstein, Harvey Kurtzman, and the rest of the EC staff.

In 1974, he opened The Million Year Picnic, one of the first specialty comic book stores in America with Chuck Wooley (later partnering with Barbara Boatner). In 1975, he opened The Science Fantasy Book Store with Mr. Wooley, in Harvard Square in Cambridge, Massachusetts. During this time, Boatner Norton Press published the influential *R. Crumb Checklist*, and Jay Kennedy's *The Official Underground and New Wave Comix Price Guide*.

By 1989, Weist was developing his ties to Sotheby's, and in 1991, the inaugural Comic Books and Comic Art auction at Sotheby's took in over a million dollars in sales. From 1991 through 2001, Mr. Weist mounted ten live auctions for Comic Books and Comic Art at Sotheby's including two MAD auctions, and two science fiction auctions, for total sales of over 15 million dollars. The important Sam Moskowitz Science Fiction Collection and the successful MAD ABOUT MAD sales were included with these auctions. Weist is also the author of *The Comic Art Price Guide*, the primary guide for important original comic art. He recently authored the Hugo-nominated *Bradbury: An Illustrated Life* for Harper Collins, and is beginning work on three other science fiction historical works including a book about Forrest J. Ackerman.

Today Mr. Weist tries to keep up with his two sons Ian and Eric, works with his wife Dana Hawkes, Sotheby's former Director of Collectibles, and mounts "Event" auctions on e-BAY for Comic Books and Comic Art, and science fiction. Weist still consults for Sotheby's and keeps busy by expanding his collection of science fiction artwork and first editions.

JIM STERANKO is one of the most controversial figures in pop culture, with a dozen successful careers to his credit. While most artists struggle for a lifetime to evolve a personal idiom, Steranko literally morphs his style with each assignment, not as variations, but radical, new approaches! He flunked high-school art classes, yet mastered techniques so diverse it seems impossible to believe that the man who created the SHIELD techno-thrillers for Marvel; the psycho-architectonic *Outland* film adaptation; the Harlan Ellison 3-D TICKTOCKMAN *Portfolio*; the panoramic SUPERMAN 400 epic; the cinematic *Red Tide*; and more than 5,000 *Prevue Magazine* pages are even the same individual!

The anomaly is compounded by a series of kaleidoscopic careers as a musician (he gigged with Bill Haley in the early days of rock 'n' roll and put the first go-go girls onstage), a magician (who developed a multitude of revolutionary card techniques at the close-up table), a pop-culture lecturer (his two volumes of *The History of Comics* have sold more than 100,000 copies each and are still the definitive resource of the four-color chronology), a filmmaker (Steven Spielberg, George Lucas, and Francis Ford Coppola chose him to collaborate on some of their most popular movies), an escape artist (his death-defying performances inspired the character Mister Miracle and the protagonist of *The Amazing Adventures of Kavalier & Clay* and more—photographer, carnival pitchman, ad agency art director, sideshow fire-eater, male model, typographer, stand-up comic, designer, publisher...the list goes on. *Wizard* recently named him the Fifth Most Influential Artist of All Time. As the writer-artist of SHIELD, CAPTAIN AMERICA, and X-MEN, he generated more than 100 innovations never seen previously in comics, then painted a multitude of movie posters, record albums, and book covers, including 30 SHADOW paperbacks. As the editor-publisher of the international newsstand entertainment magazine *Prevue*, he conducted hundreds of superstar interviews and penned more than three million words.

Steranko's work has been exhibited at 200 international exhibitions (including in the Louvre and Spain's 2002 Semana Negra cultural arts festival with an attendance of 1,000,000) and his originals have hammered at major auction houses for $20,000. Recently, he was given the 2003 Julie Award for his Lifetime Contribution to the Fantastic Arts and served as creative consultant for the History Channel's two-hour documentary *Comic-Book Superheroes Unmasked*. And he's still the best-dressed man in comics.